P9-CEU-626

THE SIBERIAN HUSKY

Lorie Long

The Siberian Husky

Project Team
Editor: Stephanie Fornino
Copy Editor: Joann Woy
Design: Stephanie Krautheim
Series Design: Stephanie Krautheim and Mada Design
Series Originator: Dominique De Vito

T.F.H. Publications
President/CEO: Glen S. Axelrod
Executive Vice President: Mark E. Johnson
Publisher: Christopher T. Reggio
Production Manager: Kathy Bontz

T.F.H. Publications, Inc.
One TFH Plaza
Third and Union Avenues
Neptune City, NJ 07753

Copyright © 2007 by T.F.H. Publications, Inc

All rights reserved. No part of this publication may be reproduced, stored, or transmitted in any form, or by any means electronic, mechanical or otherwise, without written permission from T.F.H. Publications, except where permitted by law. Requests for permission or further information should be directed to the above address.

ISBN 978-0-7938-3647-5

Printed and bound in China
08 09 10 11 12   5 7 9 8 6 4

Library of Congress Cataloging-in-Publication Data
Long, Lorie.
  The Siberian husky / Lorie Long.
    p. cm.
  ISBN 978-0-7938-3647-5 (alk. paper)
  1. Siberian husky. I. Title.
SF429.S65L66 2007
636.73--dc22
                              2006039773

This book has been published with the intent to provide accurate and authoritative information in regard to the subject matter within. While every reasonable precaution has been taken in preparation of this book, the author and publisher expressly disclaim responsibility for any errors, omissions, or adverse effects arising from the use or application of the information contained herein. The techniques and suggestions are used at the reader's discretion and are not to be considered a substitute for veterinary care. If you suspect a medical problem consult your veterinarian.

The Leader In Responsible Animal Care For Over 50 Years!®
www.tfh.com

TABLE OF CONTENTS

HISTORY

of the Siberian Husky

Imagine life in the Arctic coastal region of northeastern Siberia, one of the most extreme and inhospitable climates in the world, where winter temperatures plummet to more than −100°F (−73.3°C) and winds howl at more than 100 mph (160.9 kmh). The Chukchi, one of several indigenous tribes of the region, inhabited this land more than 3,000 years ago. A primitive village people, the Chukchi lived in permanent settlements along the coast. In this environment, where mere survival was a challenge of daily life, the Chukchi developed a breed of dog that was the progenitor of the contemporary Siberian Husky and a key to the tribe's subsistence and culture.

EARLY DEVELOPMENT OF THE SIBERIAN HUSKY

Seal and fish were the main food source for the Chukchi people, and using teams containing as many as 20 dogs, a Chukchi hunter traveled many miles (km) in a single day to hunt and ice fish. To bring their catch back to the village, the Chukchi needed a dog who could pull a light to moderately heavy load quickly and over long distances, while using a minimum amount of energy and requiring a minimum amount of food. If their dogs used less energy to do their work, the animals would have much more energy to handle exposure to extremely cold temperatures for an extended period of time.

The Chukchi dogs' temperament proved equally as important as their physical characteristics. In fact, the

The Siberian Husky's legendary sweet temperament finds its roots in his ancestor, the Chukchi sled dog.

legendary sweetness of the Siberian Husky temperament finds its roots in the easygoing and intelligent nature of these original Chukchi sled dogs. Aside from the need to be able to cooperate as members of a team, the dogs had to be eager to work and capable of enduring long days of hard labor. They required the intelligence and independent thinking necessary to "read" the condition of the ice and the terrain, helping to guide the sled even when hidden dangers in the route, like cracks in the ice, were not apparent to their handler. They needed common sense and levelheadedness to pull a load reliably and keep from constantly entangling themselves in the lines of the sled. And above all, the most desirable dogs had to be filled with a deep instinct and desire to run with sensible speed and almost endlessly.

The culture and religious ceremonies of the Chukchis reflected the extent to which they valued their dogs. They believed that two of their "husky" dogs guarded the gates of heaven and turned away anyone who had shown cruelty to a dog during his lifetime. According to a Chukchi legend, the tribe experienced a great famine that decimated both the human and dog populations of the tribe. To ensure the survival of the breed, the last two remaining puppies were nursed at a tribeswoman's breast.

To ensure that only the best dogs would be bred, the women of the tribe reared the pups after selecting which ones to keep from the litters. They discarded all but the most promising female pups and neutered all but the most promising male dogs. The men trained the dogs to pull the sleds, mostly using the neutered dogs.

Because of their affectionate and easygoing nature, the dogs slept inside the family shelters and served as companions for the children, unlike the dogs bred by other Arctic tribes. The Chukchi dogs were much too agreeable to work as guard dogs for the family. Instead, they were important members of the family group.

In the summer, the tribe released all the dogs, allowing them to feed themselves by hunting in packs for small animals. The dogs who survived the summer season returned to the village when the snow began to fall again and food grew scarce. During the winter, the handlers tied up most of the dogs when they were not working, but the few notable males who were not neutered were permitted to breed at will. Only the highest quality male dogs sired the next generation of sled dogs.

The isolation of the Chukchi people ensured that their culture remained relatively unchanged over many centuries, and their dogs maintained their purity of breed. In the nineteenth century, Russian troops pushed ever farther north toward the Arctic in search of new areas to exploit for fur trading. The spears and arrows of the primitive Chukchi and other tribal groups offered little resistance to the advanced weaponry of the invading Russian army. Accustomed to the harsh weather and able to outrun the Russian troops thanks

The Siberian's ancestors were valued for their common sense and levelheadedness.

The American Kennel Club (AKC)

Established in 1884, the AKC is the largest not-for-profit purebred dog registry in the United States. AKC registration indicates that a dog, his parents, and his ancestors are purebred. However, AKC registration does not guarantee the quality of a specific dog; it merely indicates the dog's purebred status. Nearly 2 million dogs are entered in AKC conformation shows annually, where licensed judges evaluate breeding stock.

to their swift sled dogs, the Chukchi evaded the Russian army for years before confronting them in a final battle. Using only spears, arrows, sharpened bones, and rocks, the Chukchi trapped the Russian troops in a mountain pass and won the encounter. Eventually, Czarist Russia signed a treaty with the Chukchi, who later became known as the "Apaches of the North," granting them their independence.

THE SIBERIAN HUSKY IN THE UNITED STATES

At the end of the nineteenth century, Alaskan traders discovered the fabled Chukchi dogs and imported them into the United States' Northwest Territory, naming them "Siberian Husky." This important event saved the breed from extinction in Siberia. After the Communist regime overthrew the Russian monarchy in the early 1900s, the Soviets attempted to eliminate all remnants of the former "elitist" aspects of Russian life. They advanced into Chukchi territory and determined that their fine dogs and strong tribal leaders hindered the advance of collectivization in the region. The Soviets killed many village elders, who had maintained the highest quality sled dog breeding programs, and established their own breeding plan for a much larger dog capable of hauling heavy loads of furs and other freight. Not many years passed before the Chukchi dog had essentially disappeared from Siberia.

The Siberian Husky in Alaska

Before the Soviets set their sights on the destruction of the Chukchi dogs of Siberia, the reputation of these wiry sled dogs had traveled throughout North America. The world

The Siberian's Humble Beginnings

Most purebred dog breeds arrive in America after having become popular and well established in their country of origin, and with some fanfare. The Siberian Husky quietly entered the United States in the early part of the twentieth century, in Alaska, where the locals remained unimpressed until the breed demonstrated its incredible sledding skills. Now, the Siberian is one of the most admired show and performance breeds in the country.

had become interested in polar exploration, and dogsledding in Alaska had evolved from a form of transportation during the Gold Rush to a sport for the adventurous outdoorsmen who had journeyed north in search of fame and fortune. The dogs used in the early sled-dog races were mostly Alaskan sled dogs, a larger and stronger dog than the Chukchi dogs and originally bred to haul heavy loads of freight.

Sled-dogs races provided an opportunity for some exciting competition in an otherwise grim world of relentless cold and deprivation. Frontiersmen gambled on the outcome of the races and bragged about the results. School children enjoyed a holiday from their classes during the running of the races.

In search of quality sled dogs, these adventurers traveled to the annual Markova Fair, held on the Siberian peninsula, and the site of much trading among local tribes and sled drivers from afar. In 1908, a Russian fur trader named William Goosak brought a team of Chukchi dogs to Alaska and entered his team in the 1909 All Alaska Sweepstakes sled race, organized by the newly formed

By the early 1900s, dogsledding in Alaska had evolved from a form of transportation to a sport.

9

Nome Kennel Club. The race ran from Nome to Candle, a distance of 408 miles, and offered a prize of $10,000. The trail consisted of a wide range of conditions and terrain. When Goosak and his team arrived with his Chukchi dogs for the start of the race, the locals dubbed his dogs "Siberian rats" due to their small size in comparison to the more commonplace large, freighting sled dogs. Laughed at by the other sled drivers and given little chance to win by the gamblers, Goosak hired a professional sled driver named Thurstrup, a Norwegian, to drive his team. Unfamiliar with the Chukchi style of sledding, and having made several poor tactical decisions, Thurstrup and the Chukchi team finished the race in third place. However, the speed, enthusiasm, and efficiency of Goosak's team astounded everyone connected with the race. A young Scottish miner and sportsman, Fox Maule Ramsey, chartered a schooner and sailed across the Bering Sea to Siberia the following summer to purchase about 50 Chukchi sled dogs. He sent one of his hired mushers, John Johnson, back to Siberia in 1911 to bring back more dogs. Ramsey split his new Siberian Husky dogs into three teams for the 1910 All Alaska Sweepstakes. His teams finished in first, second, and fourth places. The winning team, driven by John "Ironman" Johnson, finished in the record time of 74 hours, 14 minutes, 37 seconds. The Siberian Husky was no longer a laughing matter.

Mushers refined their working harnesses and sleds into more lightweight racing versions, which further accommodated the smaller Siberian Huskies. Sled-dog racing evolved into a more serious sport, and the popularity of the Siberian Husky became firmly established in the United States.

The Siberian Husky in New England

On the East Coast of the United States, Arctic fisherman Leonhard Seppala met Arthur Walden from New Hampshire. Walden had been winning dogsled races in New England and eastern Canada with his own line of sled dogs developed from a single, large, Mastiff-type, mixed-breed dog named Chinook. Sled racing enthusiasts considered the Walden team to be unbeatable.

Seppala entered his Siberian Husky team in a race at Poland Spring, Maine, in 1927. In a repeat of the circumstances of the dogs' debut in Nome, the Siberian team amused the New Englanders as the two teams prepared for the race. The Chinook dogs weighed 90 to 100 pounds (40.8 to 45.4 kg) each, and the Siberians weighed about 40 to 50 pounds (18.1 to 22.7 kg) each. Some spectators deemed the racing of these small sled dogs to be an inhumane act. However, today's dog breeders and mushers know that if you double the size of a dog, you only increase the dog's heart

The Story of Balto

An Arctic fisherman named Leonhard Seppala and his Siberians gained national prominence in the famous "Serum Run" that saved the city of Nome from a diphtheria epidemic in January 1925. The disease spread throughout the community and overwhelmed local supplies of serum. The closest life-saving serum was located more than 600 miles (965.6 km) away, and Nome was not yet served by the Alaskan railroad. Seppala agreed to collect the serum by dogsled and return it to Nome. After traveling nearly 170 miles (273.6 km), many of them in blizzard conditions, Seppala, with his great lead dog "Togo," met the relay team and immediately headed back to Nome with the serum. Seppala journeyed nearly 340 miles (547.2 km) over some of the most treacherous terrain in Alaska. A team driven by Gunnar Kaasen and his lead dog "Balto" completed the last leg of the relay.

A statue of Balto stands in New York City's Central Park to acknowledge all the sled dogs who participated in the Serum Run of 1925, which was a race against death. Togo became permanently lame from that run, but when he visited New York City with Seppala, he received a medal honoring his contribution to the serum relay. The modern Iditarod Trail sled-dog race from Anchorage to Nome commemorates Seppala's historic Serum Run with Togo and his courageous sled-dog team. The entire course spans more than 1,100 miles (1,770.3 km).

and lung capacity by about 30 percent. Big dogs tire much more easily than do medium-sized dogs, and they require longer rest periods. The Seppala team of Siberian Huskies easily won the race.

Seppala established a Siberian Husky kennel in Maine, with Elizabeth Ricker, a New England musher and fan of the Siberians. Their kennel supplied many teams in the area. In addition, Ricker contracted with a fur trader for the acquisition of eight additional Chukchi dogs from the North Cape of Siberia. Of the three dogs who survived the trip to Maine, Kreevanka and Tserko were foundation dogs for the gene pool of the Siberian Husky in America.

In 1932, Seppala participated in a demonstration sled-dog race at the Winter Olympics in Lake Placid, New York. Later, after the Seppala/Ricker kennel had closed, Seppala left his remaining dogs with Harry Wheeler in Quebec, who used the suffix "Seppala" in his kennel name. All of today's Siberian Huskies registered by the American Kennel Club (AKC) can trace their ancestry to dogs from

The American Kennel Club officially recognized the Siberian Husky in 1930.

the Seppala-Ricker kennel or the Harry Wheeler kennel.

AKC RECOGNITION

The Chukchi dogs who came to Nome in the early 1900s varied in phenotype, although all were of moderate proportions. Some were relatively long and leggy; others were more short-coupled and heavier boned. Some of the dogs carried symmetrical markings, and others appeared randomly marked. The Chukchi valued the working abilities of their dogs and cared little about the dogs' aesthetics. However, Seppala began breeding with the purpose of applying greater uniformity to the Siberian Husky breed, and other early breeders also wanted to create a standard of conformation for the dogs.

In 1930, the AKC officially recognized the Siberian Husky and published the first standard for the breed in April of 1932. It closely resembles the standard applied by the AKC today.

The establishment and development of the New England-bred Siberian Husky recognized by the AKC owes its origins to three influential kennels: Milton and Eva Seely's Chinook Kennels, Nicholas and Lorna Demidoff's Monadnock Kennels, and Marie Lee Frothingham's Cold River Kennels. Not only did these kennels produce top-winning show dogs, but they fielded some of the top racing teams of their time, demonstrating the elegant interaction of form and function in the Siberian Husky. Mrs. Seely and Mrs. Demidoff ranked among the top women sled-dog drivers of the time, and their teams contained many show champions.

Siberians in World War II

The United States Army used Siberian Huskies during World War II for search and rescue work in the Arctic. After the end of the war, the breed retained its popularity in the States until renewed interest in sled-dog racing ensured its bright future as a well-respected and desirable dog breed.

Chinook Kennels

Eva and Milton Seely served as founding members of the Siberian Husky Club of America (SHCA). Eva continued to judge, breed, and drive her dogs for decades after Milton's death in 1944. After Eva died in 1985, the state of Vermont named Chinook Kennels an official historic landmark of the state. Ch. Alyeska's Suggen of Chinook and Ch. Wonalancet's Baldy of Alyeska proved to be very influential foundation dogs from this kennel.

Monadnock Kennels

Lorna Demidoff's Ch. Monadnock's Pando was, arguably, the most influential stud dog in the history of the breed. When he was shown for the last time in Philadelphia, at age 14, he received a standing ovation. Later, he was discovered to be the progenitor of 100 of the 103 Siberians shown that day. He and his son, Ch. Monadnock's King, spearheaded the black-and-white coat and blue eyes that have emerged as the fashionable look of the breed. Demidoff contributed to establishing the consistency of the confident, friendly temperament valued by Siberian Husky breeders and owners today. Until her death in 1993, she remained one of the most respected Siberian judges in America.

Cold River Kennels

Marie Lee Frothingham focused on racing, and she fielded some of the most competitive Siberian Husky teams from 1936 to 1956.

The Siberian Husky has a long history of service and companionship to humankind.

The Siberian Husky Club of Great Britian (SHCGB)

The SHCGB represents the interests of the breed in the United Kingdom and welcomes members interested in the breed, whether or not they own a Siberian Husky. The club offers conformation shows, working rallies, judging seminars, and health sessions, including testing Siberians for eye and hip disorders. During the winter months, the club hosts trail races and encourages novices to observe and participate in the action. There's nothing like experiencing the energy of more than 200 very noisy sled dogs preparing to run the trail! Of course, the sociable nature of the Siberian makes for great interactions with his fans after the race is finished.

Ch. Helen of Cold River was a great racing leader and also became a noteworthy show champion. When Frothingham retired, she passed her dogs on to her team trainer to form the foundation for the renowned Marlytuk Kennels.

Alaskan Kennels

In 1946, when Natalie Jubin Norris arrived in Alaska with two AKC-registered Siberians from Chinook Kennels, no one was breeding pure Siberians. Norris' Chinook's Aladdin of Alyeska emerged as the chief foundation stud dog of purebred Siberians produced in Alaska. A tremendously skilled worker with beautiful conformation, Alaskan mushers remember this dog for his racing prowess.

Earl and Natalie Norris founded the oldest Siberian Husky kennel in Alaska—Alaskan Kennels. An Aladdin grandson, Ch. Bonzo of Anadyr, C.D., became the first Siberian Husky to win Best in Show at an AKC all-breed dog show in 1955. The Norrises have fielded many Iditarod Trail sled-dog race teams.

SIBERIAN HUSKY BREED CLUBS

The AKC maintains the official registration records for purebred dogs in the United States. Each of the registered breeds has a specific national breed club that maintains the standards of the breed and serves as a facilitator and representative for activities among the AKC, local breed clubs, and owners of the particular breed that the club supports.

Founded in 1938, the Siberian Husky Club of America (SHCA) is the AKC-recognized national breed club for the Siberian Husky,

The term "husky" is a corruption of the term "esky," a slang word for "Eskimo." "Husky" referred to the large, thick-coated, brush-tailed sled dogs of Alaska. To differentiate the new, smaller imports arriving from Siberia, the Siberian dogs became known as the "Siberian Husky," although their smaller, finer stature is not in keeping with today's common definition of the word "husky."

sometimes known as the parent club for this breed. Included in its membership are established breeders, exhibitors, fanciers, and sled-dog racing enthusiasts. Siberian Husky dogs and owners of the breed have no greater ally, mentor, and protector than the SHCA. The club is dedicated to the preservation and perpetuation of the Siberian Husky as a sound, capable, and natural breed whose characteristics of mind and body make him not only a beautiful dog and a willing worker, but also a devoted and delightful companion. The SHCA stands as an invaluable resource to the Siberian Husky community.

According to its constitution, the objectives of the SHCA include:

- Perfect the natural qualities of the purebred Siberian Husky through selective breeding.
- Encourage and support the organization of local Siberian Husky clubs as required by fanciers of the breed.
- Educate members and urge breeders to adhere to the AKC-approved standard of the breed.
- Protect and advance the interests of the breed.
- Conduct events under the rules of the American Kennel Club.

The SHCA strives to perfect the natural qualities of the purebred Siberian Husky.

With his long history of service and companionship to humankind, the Siberian Husky has developed, and continues to maintain, a loyal following of advocates, breeders, dog-sports enthusiasts, and pet dog owners. It is difficult to observe this elegant, naturally primitive, and highly athletic breed of dog without joining his expansive group of admirers. While representing the essence of the far northern lifestyle, the Siberian Husky continues to capture the hearts and minds of his many fans around the globe.

CHARACTERISTICS
of the Siberian Husky

The Siberian Husky Club of America (SHCA) first set forth the official standard for the breed during the 1930s. At the time, members drew up a standard that would allow them to show their racing sled dogs in the United States in American Kennel Club (AKC) events. They did their best to picture in words the racing Siberians to whom they were so devoted. The latest version of the standard, effective since November 1990, adheres to the principles and clarity of the original Siberian Husky standard. The AKC standard for the breed does not describe a show dog; instead, it details a medium-sized northern dog capable of performing his specific work in harness.

PHYSICAL APPEARANCE: A STRIKINGLY BEAUTIFUL DOG

The shape of the head and muzzle of the Siberian Husky, as well as his overall appearance, suggest a wolf-like, wild canid, which sometimes engenders thoughts of aggression or lack of domestication in an observer. The word "husky" in his name suggests a large, heavy dog. Nothing could be farther from the truth in either case. As mentioned in Chapter 1, the word "husky" is a corruption of the slang word "esky," used to refer to Eskimos in Alaska, and is not meant as a description of the Siberian's appearance, which is that of a moderately built, wiry animal.

Overall Look

People often confuse the Siberian Husky with the Alaskan Malamute, who is a much larger and heavier dog than the Siberian. People also often mistake Siberians who have a predominately white coat with the Samoyed, another Nordic breed. Occasionally, completely white Siberians do exist, but Samoyeds guard and herd flocks of grazing animals. Bred for a job that is very different from the work of the Siberian, the Samoyed temperament remains more assertive than the easygoing demeanor of the Siberian Husky.

The Siberian Husky is, first and foremost, an athlete. A Siberian should give the

The Siberian Husky is a moderately built, wiry animal.

impression that he can run all day long, pulling a sled containing a light to moderate load. All parts of the dog should flow together when he is in motion, creating a unified, graceful picture of efficient movement. No part of the dog's physique should be exaggerated or assault the eye at first look.

"Form follows function" is the law of canine structure. The form of the Siberian should support his function of pulling light loads at moderate speed over great distances. Quick and light on his feet, he moves freely and without the heavy appearance of carrying excess weight. Everything about the description of the desired physical construction of the Siberian suggests moderation in all aspects except style. A medium-sized, moderately compact dog, the Siberian reflects a balance of speed, power, and endurance.

Although the Siberian has enjoyed much acclaim for his achievements in Arctic exploration and sled racing, these tasks do not require bulkiness of muscle or extra weight. Any tendency toward clumsy or heavy movement indicates a dog who cannot keep pace with his team. A dog with an overly refined conformation lacks the necessary pulling power and stamina to contribute to the work of the team.

Size and Proportion

Togo, Leonhard Seppala's courageous lead dog and hero of the Serum Run in Alaska, weighed only 48 pounds (21.8 kg). Indeed, the size of the Siberian suits the dog perfectly to his task of pulling light to moderate loads for long distances.

Male Siberians should weigh 45 to 60 pounds (20.4 to 27.2 kg), and females should weigh 35 to 50 pounds (15.9 to 22.7 kg). In a group of Siberians entered in a dog show, the larger specimens of the breed stand out simply because of their size. However, the community of Siberian judges and breeders does not favor a larger dog. Most Siberian breeders insist on maintaining the moderate proportions of their breed. As a result, Siberian Huskies have avoided many of the structural problems founds in those breeds in which greater size is preferable, including hip dysplasia and osteochondritis.

Head

Some dog fanciers argue that a purebred dog's head represents a fashionable or aesthetic look desired for the breed by the current crop of dog show judges and breeders, and has little to do with the actual functioning of the breed at work. Not so for the Siberian Husky.

The medium-sized head and medium-length neck described in the standard are optimal for endurance. The well-proportioned head and neck help the Siberian maintain proper balance and control over the movement of his shoulders and front legs.

Ears

The breed standard established by the AKC calls for a well-furred ear, which protects it from the Arctic cold. The Siberian's smaller ear, compared with the German Shepherd Dog's large ear, for example, has less surface area, making it less vulnerable to the cold. The erect ear, which allows fresh air and sunlight to enter and keeps the interior drier, is less prone to infection.

Eyes

The frontal bones and the cheekbones of the canine head offer the most protection to an almond-shaped eye, which fits nicely into the canine skull. The standard for the Siberian Husky calls for an almond-shaped eye, the eye shape found most frequently among

What's in a Name?

Often, people refer to any dog with a bushy or curly tail, a thick, double coat, and prick ears as a "Husky" or "Husky mix." Most of these dogs are entirely unrelated to the purebred Siberian Husky. Therefore, aficionados of the breed refer to their dogs as either "Siberian Huskies" or "Siberians," never just "Huskies."

The Siberian's medium-sized head and medium-length neck are optimal for endurance.

wild canids. The official description of the Siberian is one of the few AKC breed standards that allows for a blue eye color. Brown eyes, blues eyes, or parti-colored eyes (one eye of each color) are all acceptable according to the Siberian standard.

Muzzle

The medium length of the Siberian muzzle describes a dog without excessive or exaggerated facial features. A long or very deep muzzle, like the Wolfhound's or the Saluki's, appears regal, impressive, and aloof. A shortened muzzle, like the Boxer's or the Bulldog's, doesn't properly warm incoming frigid air and will not support the ease of breathing necessary for load pulling over long distances. Therefore, the Siberian's medium-length muzzle contributes to his performance capabilities while keeping his expression "friendly, interested, and even mischievous" but not at all pompous or removed.

Neck, Back, and Body

The Siberian Husky should carry his neck slightly forward when he is moving, propelling him in the direction of travel. When he moves, his head should not bob up and down, which wastes energy.

For an endurance dog, a deep chest is critically important, because it houses the dog's hard-working heart and lungs. The proper depth of chest must be maintained well back along the dog's body and not sweep upward in front of the loin too quickly, or the shortened chest will diminish the capacity of the heart and lungs.

Although a broad chest also provides comfortable housing for the heart and lungs, it will impede the full follow-through of the front legs and inhibit the free-flowing gait required for long-distance travel. Thus, the standard for the Siberian Husky denotes a deep chest with ribs well-sprung but flat on the sides. A Siberian with a "barrel chest" will not exhibit proper gait because his broad chest will prevent his front legs from achieving full range of motion.

The Siberian's back should appear level but will

What Is a Breed Standard?

The standard is a written description of the ideal specimen of that breed. It addresses every aspect of the dog, including type (appearance and impression), structure, gait or movement, and temperament.

The official standard for any dog breed usually originates with the breed's parent club, not with the AKC. The membership of the parent club approves the standard for its breed and submits it to the AKC for approval.

The standard does not represent an actual dog but rather the concept of the "perfect" dog of that breed. Of course, dogs are not perfect, so a dog show judge must decide which animal presented in the ring most closely approaches perfection. Judges also must take into account the spirit of the standard by understanding the basis for its written words. With the Siberian Husky, judges study the dog's compliance with the breed standard as well as evaluate his ability to do his intended work, which is the basis and spirit of the standard.

actually be slightly higher at the withers than at the croup, but with another slight rise at the croup. These tiny rises in the spine add strength to those parts of the spine where the front and rear portions of the skeleton connect into it, and help to deliver the momentum from the thrust of the rear leg muscles to the entire skeleton. Even with these slight rises in the topline of the dog, the visual impression of the Siberian's back is that of a level topline that allows the transfer of momentum from the rear to the front of the dog to occur directly and efficiently in the line of travel.

Tail

The standard for all other Nordic breeds calls for a tail that either curls up onto the dog's body or around itself. Not so for the Siberian Husky. In the Arctic, the Siberian covered his face with his straight, thick, and brushy tail while he slept in subzero temperatures and falling snow.

Not just a decoration, the Siberian's tail carriage indicates a great deal about the condition of the muscles along his spine. A tail that touches the back of the dog or that falls to one side or the other may signal poor muscling. Because the muscles that control the carriage of the tail also influence the forward propulsion of the dog, it is likely that muscles that do not properly support the Siberian's tail will not properly do their job of moving the dog efficiently. A dog who tucks his tail tightly under his body may indicate an improperly shy temperament in that dog.

A medium-length brush of hair covers the tail. Excessive hair, or plumes, on the tail is not consistent with the rest of the Siberian's moderately long coat.

A well-tempered Siberian who runs efficiently will exhibit the desired tail set and carriage described in the standard. Indeed, the Siberian tail tells the tale of the performance capabilities of the entire dog.

Forequarters

Although this portion of the standard describes the standing dog, the requirements of the standard are based upon the necessities of body structure that support movement. The set of a dog's shoulder blades clearly indicates how the standing animal is likely to move. The standard for the Siberian describes an upper arm that angles slightly backward from shoulder to elbow and

The tail should be covered with a medium-length brush of hair.

faults a shoulder angle that is perpendicular to the ground. A properly angled shoulder allows for maximum shock absorbency when the dog is moving. It also allows for the maximum reach of the dog's legs while in motion and for full follow-through of the legs from front to back.

Widely spaced front legs will not deliver the smoothness of action and long-term endurance required of the Siberian. A narrow front indicates an insufficient breadth of chest for the job of pulling loads. Therefore, the standard for the Siberian Husky calls for moderate spacing of the front legs to sustain speed and endurance.

The leg bones of the Siberian are considerably lighter than are the bones of a Malamute, slightly lighter than the larger Golden Retriever, but slightly heavier than the Collie's. A longer leg than required by the standard would be useful to a sprinter but not an endurance runner, and a shorter leg than described by the standard would make the dog too slow and plodding. Therefore, a leg just slightly longer than the depth of the body, as described in the standard, fits the work of the Siberian perfectly.

Because feet play a fundamental role in the function of any working dog, Siberian breeders maintain a foot that is compact

Siberian Life Span

The skeletal and muscle development of a medium-sized dog becomes complete at 18 months to 2 years of age, when your dog reaches adulthood. Be sure to select age-appropriate exercises for your Siberian youngster that do not strain or tax his immature muscles and frame.

Many canine health care professionals consider a dog's senior years to begin at about eight years of age. Owners of senior dogs should carefully ensure that their dog receives proper rest after hard physical exertion, and they should become watchful for signs of joint pain. However, a hale and hearty Siberian Husky of senior status may be all but indistinguishable from younger dogs in his activity level and physical prowess.

You can enjoy the active companionship of your Siberian Husky for at least ten years, provided he receives quality health care, good nutrition, and plenty of exercise.

to prevent snow and ice from collecting between the toes and pads. Well-furred and thickly cushioned pads also benefit the performance of the feet when pulling a sled in harsh conditions. Any clumsiness or splayed toes that collect ice and subject the foot to bruising or injury will inhibit the proper functioning of the Siberian's feet. Feet are where the entire conformation of the dog finally meets the ground, and feet are the first thing to break down in a hard-working dog.

Hindquarters

The hindquarters of the dog generate the power for pulling and the speed of travel. The Siberian requires a well-muscled thigh to produce the greatest amount of forward thrust and a hock joint set low to the ground, which provides long-range endurance capabilities.

Coat

Other Arctic breeds, like the Malamute and the Samoyed, have longer and shaggier coats than the Siberian. Unique among the northern breeds, the Siberian standard calls for a coat of medium length. The difference in coat length stems from the difference in the climates in which each of these breeds originated. In the case of the Siberian, the specific conditions of climate and terrain found in his homeland made the formation of ice balls in a long, shaggy coat an ever-present danger. Thus, the Chukchis' dogs developed a coat that could withstand the Arctic cold but would prevent the collection of ice balls in their hair. A coat length of 1 to 3 inches (2.5 to 7.6 cm) is considered acceptable for the Siberian, as long as the length of the hair does not obscure the outline of the dog, and the texture of the coat is coarse and straight.

The Siberian sports a "double" coat, or a soft undercoat supporting a coarse but smooth-lying outer coat. The Siberian sheds his coat very profusely. Siberian owners deal with dog hair produced and shed at a great rate, sometimes during multiple, extended shedding seasons.

In the show ring, trimming of the fur on any part of the Siberian, except to neaten his whiskers and feet, will be penalized. Fanciers of the Siberian Husky take every measure to maintain the natural appearance of their beloved breed.

Color

Also in the interest of maintaining naturalness in the breed, the standard allows for any coat color and variation of marking. However, simply because the standard allows it does not mean

The Siberian Husky breed standard allows for any coat color and variation of marking.

Lots of Hair but Less Sneezing

The Siberian Husky cleans his coat meticulously and does not have the usual "doggy odor" associated with pet canines, even with infrequent bathing by his owner. Although this breed sheds massive amounts of hair, the coat is relatively clean and odor free. Many allergy sufferers have discovered that they can include a Siberian Husky in their family without enduring the symptoms usually caused by dog hair.

that all colors and markings are given the same weight among breeders, judges, and fanciers. As a rule of canine aesthetics, symmetry is more attractive than asymmetry. An asymmetrically marked dog, sometimes referred to as a piebald or a pinto, may have a disadvantage in the show ring over his equal who is marked symmetrically.

Two color genes determine the coat color in the Siberian Husky: black and brown/copper. Different shades of these two colors make up the foundation of all Siberian Husky coat colors. White is not considered a specific coat color but more a lack of markings or pigmentation in the coat. The depth of color created by the two color genes produces the wide range of coat colors in the breed. Breeders take into account both the color of the outer coat, or guard hairs, and the color of the undercoat when describing a particular coat color.

Black and White

Jet black: The guard coat is solid black from root to tip. Single white guard hairs may occasionally appear. The undercoat is black or dark gray. The footpads and the roof of the mouth show dark pigment.

Black: Guard hairs contain some white banding near the roots. Single white guard hairs appear more frequently. The undercoat is lighter than in the jet black dog. The dog gives the impression of being black and white but without the depth of pigment found in either jet black or white dogs.

Dilute black: Guard hairs contain a whitish cast extending from the root and tipped with black. The undercoat has a whitish cast. The dog appears to be black on the head and along the spine, with a silver effect along the flanks.

Gray and White

Silver gray: Minimal black tipping accompanies tones of white in the guard hairs, with a whitish undercoat. The dog appears silver gray on his head, back, and flanks, with only minimal darkening along the spine.

Gray: The guard hair is banded with cream or buff tones near the root, with black tipping. The light undercoat gives the dog a yellowish-gray cast.

Wolf gray: Buff tones band the guard hair near the root, with black tipping. The cream undercoat gives the dog a brownish-gray cast.

Red and White

A coppery red coat with the complete absence of black hairs, accompanied by a liver colored nose, lips, and eye rims.

Sable and White

The guard hair is banded with a reddish color near the root, and tipped with black. The undercoat is reddish-copper, and the dog's nose, lips, and eye rims are black.

Agouti and White

The guard hair is banded with black at the root and at the tip. Yellow or beige tones band the guard hairs at the center of the hair. The undercoat is very dark. Known as the "wild color," this coat color is most frequently seen in wild rodents.

Solid White

The guard hairs seem to have no bands or are banded with pale cream at the root of otherwise completely white hair. An occasional black guard hair may appear. The undercoat is solid white. This coat color results from an extreme dilution of coat pigment. The dog may have either a black or liver nose, lips, and eye rims.

Gait

Everything in the standard for the Siberian Husky leads up to the demand for a dog who is light and quick on his feet and who exhibits smooth and seemingly effortless movement. Therefore, the gaiting portion of the standard calls for the Siberian to move into a single-track gait as the speed of the dog increases. Single-tracking, a gait in which the rear legs follow in the line of the front legs, offers the greatest efficiency of movement. As the speed of the dog increases, his legs gradually angle inward until the pads of his feet fall in a single line directly under the longitudinal center of his body.

In both sexes, the Siberian must give the appearance of being capable of great endurance and sublime grace in motion.

CHARACTERISTICS OF THE SIBERIAN HUSKY

The Siberian Husky is intelligent, alert, eager to please, and adaptable to many living conditions. A versatile dog, the Siberian makes an agreeable companion for active people of all ages and with varying interests.

Companionability

Siberians are a gregarious breed and need the company of people and other dogs. Plan to include your dog in your outdoor adventures, like hiking, jogging, cross-country skiing, sledding, and vigorous outdoor play. Plan to spend time with your Siberian, and if possible, give your dog the opportunity to enjoy the company of at least one other dog.

With Children

The gregarious Siberian enjoys the company of people, making him the perfect hiking or jogging companion.

The Siberian Husky loves the company of children but is strong and powerful enough to need the supervision of an adult when children are present. Plan to monitor all interactions between your impressively rugged Siberian and young children, who may underestimate his power as a playmate.

With Strangers

The Siberian never met a stranger and is very welcoming to newcomers, despite his wolf-like appearance. A Siberian usually will not alert his owner to the approach of a stranger, which pleases the neighbors of Siberian owners who are not bothered by irritating barking every time someone passes by. If you desire the fierce loyalty of a one-person dog or the aggressive instincts of a protection dog, don't choose a Siberian.

Food Requirements

An "easy keeper," the Siberian requires a relatively small amount of food for his size, thanks to very efficient metabolism. The Chukchi developed their dogs to pull light loads at a moderate pace over long distances in low temperatures using the smallest possible amount of food. Today, the Siberian still operates fully on less food per pound (0.5 kg) of body weight than other breeds his size.

Grooming Requirements

A clean animal, the Siberian requires only basic grooming and is free of body odor. However, the density and profusion of the Siberian coat amazes everyone, including his owners. During the shedding season, which varies depending on climactic conditions, this dog releases extravagant amounts of coat that can fill bushel baskets. A brush, comb, and hardy vacuum cleaner will work overtime when a Siberians sheds his coat.

Inbred Behaviors

Take the time to evaluate the inbred behaviors (the way he has been "programmed") of the Siberian to determine if this breed will suit your particular lifestyle and the relationship you want to develop with your dog. Remember that you will work within the dog's pre-programmed set of characteristics to produce the lifelong companion whom you desire.

Digging

Siberians love to dig, both when they are puppies and when they are adults. This ancient instinct to dig can be curbed but not eliminated; it becomes less bothersome

Children and Dogs

Would you ask your third grader to drive to the store and pick up a few groceries for you? Or perhaps get dinner ready for the family by six o'clock? Why not? After all, your child has ridden in the car and accompanied you to the supermarket many times and knows all about buying groceries. She certainly has watched you prepare and serve hundreds of meals on a defined time schedule. But of course, your child does not possess the maturity, focus, or judgment required to drive a car, shop responsibly, or pull a timely meal together, even armed with recipes.

Training a puppy or dog to become a well-adjusted pet requires lots of mature thought, planning, focus, and judgment — attributes most commonly found in adults. Although a child benefits from the companionship of a well-trained dog provided by her parents, the job of producing such a dog belongs to grown-ups.

The Siberian Husky's legendary gentleness with children does not preclude the need for supervision and training when your children and dogs interact. A well-trained and properly supervised Siberian Husky brings joy to adult and young family members alike.

The Siberian is intelligent, alert, and eager to please.

when the dog can indulge this deep-seated behavior in a safe and acceptable manner at home. Siberians dug crater-like holes for protection from winter snows and the heat of the summer and still enjoy the safety and comfort of a nicely dug hole today.

Moaning and Whining

Although the Siberian rarely barks, he moans or whines, and when the mood strikes him, he will howl with his head held high. This vocalization is one of the most beautifully haunting sounds in nature. However, if the Siberian's howl is not music to your ears or to the ears of your neighbors, this isn't the dog for you.

Predatory Instincts

Predatory instincts remain strong in the Siberian. During the Arctic summer, the Chukchi allowed their dogs to roam freely and fend for themselves by hunting and eating small animals far from the village. Siberians have retained their swift, cunning, and patient hunting skills.

An Arctic hunter, the Siberian views small animals as prey rather than as playmates. Although very amiable with other dogs, the Siberian relates best to other household pets when they have been raised with those pets. If your house contains a changing universe of guinea pigs, birds, turtles, cats, or other small animals that may cross the path of your dog, don't choose a Siberian.

Roaming

A nomad at heart, the Siberian adjusts quickly to new environments and situations. However, as a wanderer, the Siberian has no homing instincts and no fear of cars, strangers, or other animals. The most dangerous attribute of a Siberian, for the pet owner, is his tremendous and deep-seated desire to run. Once loose, he can fall prey to injury and disease. He can turn into a pest that chases and hunts small animals or digs in the neighbors' gardens. For his protection, a Siberian must be kept confined or under control at all times by his owner. Restrict him to his own yard, and always walk him on a leash unless he is in a strictly controlled environment.

Running

The powerful ancestry of the sled dog still fuels the Siberian's longing to run, run, and run some more, and their conformation has given them the ability to enjoy running effortlessly, all day long. Once free to run, the Siberian will not slow down for hours. This characteristic, so important to the sled dog, presents a major safety issue in a traditional home environment. Unless an owner keeps her Siberian in a properly fenced yard or on a leash, the dog's safety is in serious jeopardy. However, catching a glimpse of a Siberian Husky running under controlled conditions is one of the sweetest sights in the world of dogs.

Inquisitiveness

The inquisitive nature of the Siberian endears the breed to its owners. This dog seeks out the source of that interesting scent, chases and hunts small animals, and is determined to discover what lurks on the other side of the fence. A primitive propensity to investigate his surroundings comes ingrained in the Siberian. To satisfy his discovery instinct, the Siberian can become a talented escape artist. Capable of crawling through small holes, scaling high fences with ease and grace, chewing through ropes, and slipping collars with great skill, the Siberian's owner must construct an escape-proof enclosure and constantly check for loose fencing, a tiny new hole, or the gleam in her dog's eye that says "I think I can get out here!" when he's in a certain section of the yard. If you cannot provide a suitable method for confining a resourceful dog who does not want to just lie in the sun all day, don't choose a Siberian.

Intelligence

The intelligence of the Siberian Husky endears people to the breed, while his independent spirit and quickness to become bored challenge his owners and require a patient and committed trainer. Not a lap dog, the Siberian Husky brims with eagerness and inquisitiveness, and he needs a family member to guide his activities and polish his manners.

Temperament

The Siberian Husky has an affectionate and delightful temperament. Their gentle disposition reflects how fully the Chukchi people incorporated their sled dogs into their own family life. Housing the dogs in the family shelter, the Chukchi encouraged their children to play with the dogs, and they employed the dogs as companions and canine "babysitters" for their children.

While the Siberian demonstrates strong affection for his family, he is not a one-person dog. The Siberian greets guests cordially, with interest, and with the proper decorum. He does not exhibit fear or suspicion of strangers or of other dogs. After all, a dog who is not able to work amiably with other dogs is a poor choice for a sled dog. Because of the Siberian's wolfish appearance, strangers unfamiliar with his hospitable temperament may consider him a threat at first meeting. However, this misunderstanding soon melts away when the stranger learns of the true nature of this friendly breed and experiences a bit of the easy-going Siberian Husky nature for himself.

Although congenial to people and dogs, the Siberian stands ready and able to defend himself and will match any aggressor with a suitable response.

The powerful ancestry of the sled dog still fuels the Siberian's longing to run.

Trainability

The Siberian willingly obeys simple commands from an owner he respects, and he acts with friendly decorum when in the company of people and other dogs. However, as a breed, Siberians do not excel in precision performance activities like advanced or competitive obedience work. If you are searching for a breed particularly for obedience work or performance work other than the natural work of the Siberian Husky, this dog is not for you.

Although the present-day Siberian has changed since his introduction into the United States in the 1900s, the breed retains the qualities so prized by the Chukchi in their Arctic sled dogs. With his stately beauty, smiling good humor, and unparalleled work ethic, the Siberian Husky attracts many potential owners who think of this breed as the ideal pet. After carefully weighing the pros and cons of owning a Siberian, you can make an educated decision about how this dog will fit into your family and lifestyle. If you still believe that the Siberian is the best breed for you, welcome to the fold of dog owners who appreciate and admire the natural beauty, talents, and working ability of their Siberians. Congratulations on your good taste and commitment to owning this challenging breed. Now, it's time to consider how you will choose your special Siberian Husky.

The Siberian demonstrates strong affection for his family.

Why Does My Dog Do What He Does?

The more you learn about the history of the Siberian Husky, including the centuries of careful, purposeful breeding behind each specimen of the breed, the more you will understand that a reason exists for the behaviors you will experience from a Siberian. Although digging holes appears to be destructive, it serves the need to make a shelter, create a storage place for food, and provide exercise. The casual indifference to commands from his owner reflects the serious weight the Siberian gives to the pecking order in his pack. Although amiable and affectionate, the Siberian will not submit easily unless sure of the leadership ability of his owner. Like his ancestors, who were guided by a skilled lead dog in the sled team, the Siberian insists on identifying a reliable leader in his family before he will offer his respect and obedience. Earning the respect of a Siberian requires constant certainty and clarity of training from his owner.

Chapter

3

PREPARING

for Your Siberian Husky

A s with most aspects of housing, handling, and training a dog, preparation and anticipation on the part of the owner reap many rewards. Once you have decided to add a Siberian Husky to your family, take the time to carefully consider all the factors involved in acquiring and caring for your new family member. In the process, you will ensure a successful transition from the dog's previous home to your home. Your puppy or adult dog will respond by acknowledging your caring leadership, and you will enjoy making your dog feel at home right away.

PRELIMINARY DECISIONS

Before you bring home your new Siberian Husky, you'll have to make a few preliminary decisions, including deciding whether a puppy or adult, or male or female will be best for your family.

Puppy or Adult?

Who can resist the eight-week-old ball of fluff romping around with his equally adorable siblings? Puppies offer their new owners a "clean slate," a chance to mold a companion or performance dog and somewhat shape the behavior of the dog. Bringing home a puppy allows the owner to experience and participate in all the fascinating stages of a dog's life.

However, clean slates do not remain clean for long. Puppies are like human children; they absorb and integrate their experiences almost faster than an owner can manage them and the behaviors that these experiences generate. Introduce life experiences, good or bad, and you get the resulting behaviors, good or bad. Repeat the same process a few times, and you get behavioral habits, good or bad, but now quite well entrenched. Understanding and staying ahead of this process ensures that

Choosing between a puppy and adult Siberian Husky is one of the first decisions that you'll have to make.

a puppy will grow into an enjoyable and well-adjusted member of the family and a well-mannered companion when away from home. Ignoring this process in the formative months of a dog's life, or giving this process minimal attention, ensures that your future with your puppy will contain many more frustrations and struggles than are necessary.

Take a serious look at your lifestyle, available time and energy, and the willingness of all the members of your family to join in the challenging process of raising a puppy. Also, be ready to spend a good deal of time preparing your home for his arrival. Learn about how to build desirable behaviors in a puppy and young dog, and monitor the interactions of the members of your household with the puppy so that you can maintain consistency in his handling.

It's fair to say that the first six to nine months of a puppy's life make the dog. Your ability to actively and knowledgeably manage and direct your dog's puppyhood will set the stage for the next 10 to 15 years. Is this challenge one that you are prepared to accept at this time, given your daily schedule, your other commitments, and your interest in developing a puppy-raising agenda? If not, consider the alternative of purchasing or adopting an adult Siberian.

Obtaining an adult dog from a responsible breeder or owner offers you the opportunity to own a dog whose foundation has been firmly established by a knowledgeable individual. Siberians, highly regarded for their adaptability and easy temperaments, can shift into a new living environment with some ease, as long as their basic requirements are met. Adult Siberians often quickly settle into a new home because they are mature enough to read and react to their surroundings successfully.

Animal shelters, foster care programs, and the Siberian Husky national rescue organization offer purebred adult Siberians for adoption. The previous owners of these dogs may have surrendered them because they claimed dissatisfaction with the dog's behavior or were incapable of meeting the dog's needs. However, most of these dogs are the victims of inadequate training and neglectful treatment and are perfectly willing to behave in an appropriate manner if given the proper education and guidance.

Think about undertaking the task of moving into a new home. At any particular time in your life, would you want to purchase property, research floor plans, work with contractors, arrange for landscaping, and select every color and feature contained in your new home to achieve a relatively custom product? Or would you rather purchase an existing home that suits you with little or no modification? If you prefer to invest your time and energy in developing a "custom" product, a puppy may be the right choice for you. If you prefer to start with an "existing structure" and work to make it your own, then an adult Siberian Husky may find his dream home with you.

If One Is Good, Are Two Better?

Resist the temptation to bring two Siberian Husky puppies home from the breeder. Although littermates at play paint a picture of joyous enthusiasm and provide nonstop entertainment, you must help your puppy make a successful transition from his former home to his new home with you. You must become your puppy's friend and leader, without vying with a littermate for his attention. If you want to own two or more Siberian Huskies, purchase a second pup a year or more after adding the first pup to your home.

*Begin your search for a
Siberian by thoroughly
researching all aspects of
the breed and its care.*

Male or Female?

Female Siberians are gentle and patient. Male Siberians are kind and willing. If you select a female Siberian, be certain that you can protect her adequately from an unwanted pregnancy during her season, or have her spayed. She will be especially warm with young children. If you select a male, plan to neuter him unless he will be a part of your breeding program. Intact males are driven to wander in search of fertile females. Many female dogs "mark" territory as religiously as male dogs.

The temperament of the particular Siberian Husky whom you add to your family and the quality of your training program will play the most important role in determining how well your Siberian Husky suits your lifestyle.

FINDING YOUR SIBERIAN HUSKY

Begin your search for a Siberian Husky by reading all the information you can find about the breed and its care. Search reputable sites on the Internet, such as the American Kennel Club (AKC) and the Siberian Husky Club of America (SHCA) websites. Collect breed information books and periodicals. Then, it's time to find an invaluable source of information about the Siberian Husky.

Inevitably, you will discover some contradictory information offered by one or another of your research sources. Much reference material will mention only the positive characteristics of the Siberian Husky, but your common sense tells you that no breed is perfect. A responsible source will honestly inform you about the Siberian Husky breed in general and about a puppy or dog in particular so that you can make informed choices along the way.

Breeders

Do your homework! Selecting a puppy or a dog launches a commitment that will span many years. Take your time, look at several kennels, and interact with more than one litter of puppies or more than one adult dog. Confirm all agreements, guarantees, prices, and historical information, such as the dog's health history, in writing. During this worthwhile process, you and your new Siberian Husky puppy or dog will discover each other and begin a relationship that will enrich you both for many years.

Locating a Breeder

You can locate a Siberian Husky breeder by accessing the breeder directory through the AKC's website. Here, you can find the dates and locations of AKC-sanctioned conformation shows where breeders exhibit their breeding stock of Siberian Huskies for evaluation by an AKC judge. You can also contact the SHCA, which operates a breeder referral service, among other important aids. In addition, some magazines published for the serious dog enthusiast contain breeder directory sections in which breeders advertise their kennels.

If you visit an AKC conformation show with the expectation of speaking with Siberian Husky breeders, remember to approach the breeders after their dogs have been judged and have exited the ring. Breeders and handlers focus on showcasing the best qualities of their dogs for the judge's inspection and require the full attention and cooperation of their dogs before they enter the ring and while under evaluation. After the judging of the breed has been completed, you will find most breeders relaxed and more than

It's important to choose a Siberian who matches your lifestyle and requirements.

happy to answer your inquiries. You will also find the dogs at ease and agreeable to interacting with you.

Visit a prospective breeder's kennel, and plan to spend time discussing how a Siberian Husky will fit into your family. Inspect her dogs, kennel facility, contracts, and other documents that will accompany a puppy or dog from this facility. If you're looking for a puppy to buy, the breeder should have at least one of the puppy's parents, either the sire or the dam, on site and available for your examination.

Buyer Screening

Plan to be carefully screened by a reputable breeder. Such a breeder must assure your suitability for owning a Siberian. It is cruel to place a Siberian in an unsuitable environment, such as a home without a secure enclosure or a home in which the owner considers outdoor exercise an undertaking to be avoided at all costs. In short, it is unethical to burden an owner with a breed of dog that does not match her lifestyle and requirements.

A responsible breeder might ask you about who will manage the dog's care and training in the home; how the dog will be confined and exercised; what dogs you have owned in the past, including how these dogs lived and died; and if all of the members of your family enthusiastically want to own a dog at this time. Don't misconstrue a breeder's questions as an insult or an intrusion. On the contrary, be wary if a breeder does not closely quiz you about your home, family, and expectations of a Siberian Husky.

Signs of a Good Breeder

Responsible breeders produce an occasional litter with the goal of improving their breed, *not* to educate their children about reproduction or simply because they happen to own two dogs of the same breed. Quality breeders usually have a waiting list of potential buyers for their puppies and older dogs and rarely resort to advertising their puppies in the newspaper or on the Internet, although they may announce a planned litter or the availability of an older dog on the breed club's Internet chat list. Be wary if a breeder has whelped a litter for a spurious reason, does not have either the sire or the dam on the premises, or has a backyard full of puppies and dogs available for purchase.

Responsible breeders actively compete with their dogs in conformation shows and in canine performance events. They may train their dogs for obedience competition, tracking events, sled-dog racing, agility trials, and other activities. These breeders contribute their time and expertise to the national and local Siberian Husky breed clubs and other organizations, like the International Siberian Husky Club (ISHC), that sponsor breed-related activities. Competition with other well-bred Siberians maintains the quality of a breeder's stock by allowing the breeder to gauge the worthiness of a dog in a variety of settings. The breeder then can assess where the dog fits into her breeding program. Be wary if a breeder does not belong to any dog organizations and does not show or compete with her dogs.

Take a Number, Please!

One of the happiest days of preparing to purchase a Siberian Husky comes when the breeder you have selected allows you to pick your puppy from the available members of the litter or introduces you to an adult dog ready for a new home. The breeder will assist you with your choices, of course, but be sure to ask her to arrange for you to interact with each prospective puppy individually. Ask her to allow you to interact with an adult dog outside of his kennel quarters and away from the breeder's other dogs. You can more clearly determine a puppy or dog's reactions to his environment, strangers, and other outside influences when you interact one-on-one with him. Then, you can more easily find a puppy or adult dog with the temperament that you desire.

Reputable breeders will eagerly explain, teach, and advise prospective owners about all aspects of the Siberian Husky. They will clearly outline the disadvantages, as well as the advantages, of owning a Siberian. They will help you to determine whether a Siberian is the right breed for you and whether you are prepared to care for a Siberian Husky for the life of the dog, not just while he's a cute puppy or a convenient adult dog. Be wary if a breeder does not fully identify the peculiarities of Siberian Huskies, as well as their many merits.

Reputable Siberian Husky breeders sell only healthy stock, fully vetted and guaranteed for a reasonable length of time after the sale, usually about one year. The dog should have been tested for any genetic deficiencies that can be detected by the age at which the breeder sells the dog. Breeders should offer puppies for sale no younger than seven weeks of age at the absolute earliest. Preferably, the breeder will release puppies at 8 to 12 weeks of age. Adult dogs should be up to date on vaccinations, especially rabies, for which a legal requirement exists, or they should have been recently titer-tested for an adequate level of protection from canine diseases, conferred by the dog's past vaccinations. Adult dogs should be free of intestinal parasites, such as worms, and external parasites, such as ticks and fleas, and they should have been cleared of the presence of heartworm disease.

Many breeders perform temperament testing on their puppies. These tests consist of exposing each puppy to a variety of challenging situations and experiences, like hearing loud noises or facing strangers wearing big hats or carrying open umbrellas. These tests attempt to predict the ultimate temperament of the puppy as an adult dog, enabling the breeder to make the best possible placements for their puppies. The breeder will document each puppy's results during the test, and she should share this information with buyers. The breeder should offer a record of veterinary treatments, testing, and vaccinations to each buyer, in writing. In addition, a breeder's own dogs should appear healthy and demonstrate the proper Siberian Husky temperament. Be wary if a breeder cannot produce complete health records for a dog or puppy, offers to sell very young puppies, or whose kennel contains dogs who appear unwell or overly shy, aggressive, or unfriendly toward human visitors.

Ethical Siberian Husky breeders retain a responsibility for each

Responsible breeders actively compete with their dogs in canine performance events.

of the dogs they breed and sell for the duration of their lives. They offer, or even require through a contractual agreement, that any dog they place must be returned to them if the buyer's situation changes and the buyer cannot keep the dog. This commitment applies whether the breeder sells a ten-week-old puppy or a ten-year-old dog. No responsible breeder wants even one of her dogs to end his life in the local animal shelter, on the streets, or shuffled from one home to another because each successive family cannot keep the dog. When a breeder receives notification that one of her dogs has lost his home, she will collect the unwanted dog, have him examined and treated by a veterinarian, update his training and socialization skills, groom the dog, and find him a new, loving home. Breeders who harbor more interest in your money than in enhancing and caring for the Siberian Husky breed will not agree to take back a puppy or dog. Be wary if a breeder acts more like a broker than a breeder and makes no mention of accepting a puppy or dog back from you if you cannot keep the dog for any reason.

Responsible breeders sell pet-quality puppies and dogs to buyers who have no intention of breeding them. These dogs may be sold with a limited AKC registration, often referred to as a nonbreeding registration. Under the limited AKC registration, the breeder provides AKC registration for the dog sold, but prohibits the AKC registration of any progeny of the dog in the future. Lovely performance and pet dogs carry limited AKC registrations. Many breeders sell limited-registration puppies and dogs on a price scale more attractive to owners who are not purchasing serious breeding stock. Be wary if a breeder seems disinterested in your plans for breeding a puppy or dog from her kennel.

One of the greatest advantages of purchasing your Siberian Husky from an experienced breeder is that a reputable breeder will remain only a phone call away for the life of your dog. Eager to stay in touch with the owners of dogs from their kennel, responsible breeders provide breed-specific information, expert advice, and ongoing assistance to owners. They care deeply about your success with the dog and know how to address problems that arise throughout your dog's lifetime. Be wary if the breeder states that all sales are final and gives you the impression that she will likely disappear from your life once she has sold you a puppy or dog.

Rescue

If you decide to adopt an adult Siberian Husky, contact Siberian Husky rescue. They may be able to connect you with a wonderful dog.

How Siberians End Up in Rescue

For a variety of reasons, good-quality Siberian Huskies find their way into the hands of the Siberian Husky rescue group. The dog's owner may have experienced a life change, like moving into a small apartment, or she may have found that this cute puppy grew into a large, continuously shedding, very active adult dog. Because most owners keep more than one Siberian, when an owner can no longer maintain her dogs, several Siberians lose their home at the same time, sending multiple dogs to the shelter or rescue group. Unfortunately, homeless Siberians constitute a growing problem for the breed club.

Siberian Husky Rescue Organizations

The SHCA has given its support to a nationwide network of Siberian Husky rescue organizations in the belief that Siberian

rescue can be worked best by volunteers operating and making decisions at a local level. Thanks to dedicated rescuers across the country, unwanted Siberian Huskies have a good chance of finding a new, caring family.

Siberian Husky rescue aids stray Siberians and removes surrendered Siberians from shelters and homes where they are no long wanted. Members of the group remain in regular contact with pounds, shelters, humane societies, and private rescue organizations to gain the cooperation of these groups, and they encourage them to contact Siberian Husky rescue when they locate an abandoned Siberian. Rescue personnel place the dogs in permanent adoptive homes or in temporary foster homes if they have not yet identified a suitable long-term home for the dog.

How Siberians Are Placed in New Homes

Many rescue personnel are Siberian Husky breeders and owners themselves, and they carefully evaluate the rescued dogs for correct temperament, health status, and the presence of desirable or undesirable traits or behaviors. They transport the dogs to and from veterinary offices and foster homes. They take the time to educate prospective owners about the breed in general and about the particular dog in their care so that they can maximize the chances of locating a suitable, permanent home for each dog. They also arrange to neuter intact Siberians before placement in a new home.

Siberian Husky rescue understands that placing rescued dogs with bad temperaments, inadequate socialization experiences, or problems resulting from careless breeding only promotes the growth of negative opinions about the breed. Therefore, the rescuers select the most adoptable Siberians for placement in a new home.

If you apply to adopt a Siberian from the rescue organization, prepare to be screened by at least one member of the rescue team. The member will conduct an interview and perform a house check to help determine if a Siberian Husky will fare well in your home. She will provide a health record and all information relating to the dog's temperament, likes and dislikes, eating habits, history with other animals, and other quirks, to the extent that the rescuer can document them. The rescue group charges adopters a fee to cover the group's expenses and requires adopters to sign an adoption

What Good Are "Papers?"

AKC registration documents alone do not guarantee the quality of a Siberian Husky puppy or dog any more than a DMV registration guarantees that a driver owns a top-quality automobile. An AKC registration merely certifies that a particular puppy or dog is the purebred offspring of two AKC-registered parents. Purchasing a puppy or a dog from a reputable source ensures the ultimate quality of the dog.

contract. This contract outlines reasonable requirements for the care of the dog in your home, along with an agreement to return the dog to the rescue group if you cannot keep him.

Thankfully, Siberians are a stable breed of dog with respect to temperament. They have the steadiness needed to withstand the emotional and physical strain of undergoing the rescue and adoption process, unlike other, more highly strung breeds.

Shelters and Adoption Centers

The animal shelter or pound may, on occasion, admit a purebred Siberian Husky to the facility. Although the shelter employees may not have the depth of knowledge about the breed that you will find from Siberian Husky breeders and from the breed rescue group, they will guide you through selecting a dog who fits your lifestyle.

Some retail pet supply chains support the adoption of homeless dogs by allowing shelters and other foster-care facilities to bring highly adoptable dogs to the store on "adoption days," when they will be exposed to shoppers and other visitors likely to offer them a good home.

Choose a Siberian Husky with a healthy physical appearance.

How Siberians Are Placed in New Homes

If you decide to adopt a Siberian Husky from a shelter, notify the staff at the shelter, or speak with them at a pet store adoption day. They will inform you of the likelihood of finding a purebred Siberian Husky through their program.

Adoption centers conduct interviews, perform home checks, require that the new owner sign an adoption agreement, and charge a small fee for their services. Usually, they can provide only a limited amount of information about the dog available for adoption, and they may possess limited knowledge about the unique characteristics of the Siberian Husky breed.

CHOOSING A SIBERIAN HUSKY

When selecting a healthy Siberian Husky, consider a variety of factors, including the dog's environment, physical appearance, and temperament.

Environment

First, check the conditions in which your candidate for adoption or purchase currently lives. If his kennel area looks and smells clean, if he has access to a supply of fresh drinking water, and if no old food is moldering in a nearby bowl, you have an indication that your potential pup has been kept in healthy conditions.

Physical Appearance

Make certain that the pup's eyes are clear and bright and that there is no discharge from the nose. Check an adult dog's teeth for a buildup of calculus and tartar, which signals inadequate dental care that may contribute to future health problems. Look into the dog's ears for signs of dark, waxy matter that suggest the presence of ear mites. Be certain that his coat is uniform in length and texture and without thin or hairless spots. Check that the coat stands out nicely from the dog's body and is not matted down. Part the coat and check the skin for evidence of fleas, skin eruptions, or excessive dryness. Watch the Siberian while he is in motion. His movement should appear completely effortless and smooth at a medium speed. Displays of stumbling, awkwardness, trouble shifting from one gait to another, or tiring quickly may indicate poor skeletal development.

Temperament

Look for a dog who approaches you willingly, with some curiosity, and without hurling himself at you or cowering from you. Notice whether he feels comfortable with other dogs present in his environment and if he behaves politely in their company. Check the puppy's reaction to strange objects and make note of any extremes in his behavior. Keep in mind that you want to match your new dog to your lifestyle. If you are looking for a gentle companion who loves children, choose a mild-mannered dog. If you are looking for a canine athlete or performance dog, select a "busier" Siberian who appears more restless than most and full of energy. Many breeders conduct comprehensive temperament tests on puppies and adult dogs, and they can help you to assess a particular dog's temperament traits.

PAPERWORK

Observe the breeder's puppies to see which one best suits your lifestyle in terms of temperament.

When you purchase a Siberian Husky puppy or adult dog from a responsible source, you will receive most or all of the following documents.

Written Sales Agreement

This contractual document specifies the price of the dog, all agreements regarding the conditions of the sale, and all guarantees provided by the breeder and the owner. If you are paying the purchase price for a show-quality Siberian Husky of breeding potential, this agreement should include information about a refund or replacement of the dog in the event that a hereditary disease or a disqualifying fault afflicts the dog in the future. Health guarantees usually require that a veterinarian examine the Siberian within several days of the sale to provide professional concurrence of the general good health of the dog.

AKC Registration Form

In the case of puppies, breeders register their litters and provide litter registration documents to each buyer, who later register the individual puppy they purchase. If the breeder has not received her litter registration material from the AKC by the time you purchase a puppy, the breeder should provide written identification of the puppy that includes a statement that the puppy is a purebred Siberian Husky, the registered names and registration numbers of the sire and dam of the puppy, complete breeder contact information, and the puppy's date of birth. The sales agreement should include a statement that the registration documents will be forwarded to the new owner as soon as possible. In no event should these documents arrive later than 90 days from the sale, unless agreed upon in advance by both parties. Breeders may provide limited AKC registration materials to buyers who purchase nonbreeding stock, such as a companion dog or a performance dog, and full AKC registration materials to buyers who purchase puppies for breeding stock. Full registration allows for the AKC registration of any puppies produced by the dog. The appropriate individual AKC registration document should accompany the sale of an adult dog.

Signed Three-Generation Pedigree

Especially in the case of show-quality dogs, this information provides input for making decisions about future breeding plans and partners. It confirms the breeding history of your Siberian's "line" should you be interested in a contribution from a specific dog, or dogs, in the makeup of your Siberian Husky.

AKC Online Registration

If you purchase your Siberian Husky puppy from a breeder who has registered the litter with the AKC, it's likely that you will be able to quickly register your individual puppy using the AKC online registration service. If you purchase your puppy directly from the breeder, with no transfers of ownership involved prior to your registration request, visit the AKC's website to start the registration process. Remember to ask for hard copies of the litter registration and the AKC dog registration application form from the breeder for your records and in the event of a problem with online registration.

Health History

This document records the dates of vaccinations for distemper, hepatitis, leptospirosis, and parvovirus, as well as the dates of treatments to eliminate worms, fleas, and ticks. For adult dogs, the health history should include information about rabies vaccinations, heartworm checks, medications administered, and the date of neutering. For intact females, look for information about when an intact female Siberian became fertile (came into season), became pregnant, and delivered puppies, if applicable. For intact males, look for a record of any breedings or attempted breedings. The health history should encompass the feeding schedule used by the breeder and may include specific instructions, such as avoiding certain foods due to allergies or other reactions.

Hereditary Disease Evaluation Results

For the adult Siberian Husky and for the parents of puppies, the breeder should provide the certification number of the genetic health screening report for the dog or dogs, or a copy of the report itself, issued by the organization that screens for the presence of a particular genetically based health problem. The Orthopedic Foundation for Animals (OFA) screens for canine hip dysplasia and other structural diseases. After studying a radiograph of the dog's hips, the OFA grades the hips with respect to the presence of dysplasia, a malformation of the hip joint, and issues a report documenting its findings. The Canine Eye Registry Foundation (CERF) produces an individual results report and maintains a registry of dogs examined by a veterinary eye specialist for the presence of inheritable eye diseases. The Siberian Husky Ophthalmic Registry (SHOR) provides a low-cost alternative to CERF evaluation for Siberian Husky breeders and owners. The dates on these reports should be within two years prior to the purchase of the puppy (for his sire and dam) or adult dog, if possible.

Puppy Temperament Testing Results

If a breeder performs temperament testing on her puppies, ask to review a copy of the test results. If you decide to purchase a puppy from a litter before the breeder has tested the puppies, ask her if you can observe selected portions of the testing.

Publications of the SHCA

The SHCA information packet for owners contains a wealth of information about the breed and the parent club. Breeders who are members of the club can provide these packets when you purchase a dog or puppy from their kennel.

HOME AT LAST

Creating the right environment for your Siberian will help your puppy or adult make a quick, contented adjustment to life in his new home. The Siberian's environment consists of several factors, including shelter and general housing, equipment that will help you to manage your dog, and resources outside of your immediate family, like pet sitters, who can help to maintain your Siberian's comfortable environment when you are away.

An Arctic breed, the Siberian thrives in very cold weather; however, he does require shelter from the elements when outdoors, such as a doghouse.

Provide your Siberian with a large, fenced yard.

General Home Preparation

A northern or Arctic breed, the Siberian Husky can remain outdoors in very cold weather. However, your Siberian requires shelter from the elements, especially from drafts and wet weather, as well as a method of exercise and containment that prevents him from running loose. A chronically wet dog becomes prone to skin problems and other diseases, thereby undermining his good health and comfort. A dog who roams the neighborhood endangers himself, children, and other animals, and soon earns the title of "neighborhood nuisance."

Fenced Yard

Provide your Siberian with a large, fenced yard. The fence should be at least 6 feet (1.8 m) tall and constructed of chain link, if possible. Constantly curious Siberians like to watch what's happening on the other side of the fence, and they occasionally become very intent on activities taking place outside their own yards. A wooden fence may not detain a determined Siberian Husky. Some breeders even recommend installing a block wall to ensure the containment of the dog.

Notorious for their delight in digging, a Siberian who cannot jump over his fence will make a steadfast effort to dig under it. Many owners bury wire in the ground at the fence line to prevent digging out. For another option, secure a length of field fence with a 2-by-4-inch (5.1-by-10.2-cm) mesh to the bottom of your yard fence, then turn it inward and lay it on the ground inside the fence. Tack it in place. Other methods include lining the perimeter of the fence with railroad ties or landscaping timbers sunk partially into the ground. Cinder blocks can fill low spots under a fence because they are too heavy for a digging Siberian to move out of the way. Blocks can also provide a perimeter barrier if they are sunk partway into the ground along the fence line. Check your fenced yard regularly for the appearance of "escape hatches" or the beginnings of dig-out spots. Repair them immediately.

Sandbox

Set up a sandbox in a shaded part of your yard, and encourage your Siberian to indulge his digging skills in the sandbox rather than on the fence line. Bury a couple of chew bones or outdoor toys in the sandbox to attract his attention to digging in that spot. Don't plant your prize-winning flowers or vegetables within the dog's fenced yard.

Chain-Link Kennel

For absolute security, a chain link kennel run provides the best option. The run should measure 6 to 7 feet (1.8 to 2.1 m) wide, 10 to 15 feet (3.0 to 4.6 m) long, and at least 6 feet (1.8 m) high. Construct the run with a concrete floor. A concrete patio block floor is easy to install, less expensive than a poured concrete slab, and often drains better than a solid concrete floor. Seal a solid concrete floor with an outdoor paint or resin finish to make the floor even easier to maintain and more sanitary. Be careful when the temperatures fall below freezing for the first time in the season. The concrete slab will become icy, and although your dog will cope, you don't want to take a fall while cleaning his run.

The roof of the kennel may consist of chain-link fencing or exterior-grade plywood. Either material should be covered with a weather-proof tarp to shade the kennel and protect your dog from the elements.

Add cedar shavings to the kennel run to absorb urine between cleanings. Scoop out wet shavings and feces daily. Completely

AKC Indefinite Listing Privilege

A purebred dog might not be eligible for AKC registration for many reasons: lost paperwork by the owner or breeder, incomplete or absent registration paperwork for a dog from a breed rescue program, an unregistered parent, and the like. If you cannot register your purebred Siberian Husky with the AKC but wish to participate in AKC-recognized athletic and performance events, apply for an AKC Indefinite Listing Privilege (ILP). An ILP allows you to enter your dog in AKC obedience trials, agility trials, tracking tests, and other events. To receive an ILP, a dog must be neutered.

remove the shavings, hose out the kennel, and replace the shavings on a regular basis.

Keep your dog in the kennel run whenever you are unable to supervise his play and exercise. Allow him to run freely in the fenced yard when you can play with him and prevent his attempts to dig in inappropriate places or to escape the yard.

Doghouse

Whether your Siberian spends his outdoor time in a fenced yard or a kennel run, he needs access to shelter in the form of a doghouse. A simple plywood cube, open on one side, offers the best solution. Build a house about 3 feet by 4 feet (0.9 m by 1.2 m) by at least 2 feet (0.6 m) high, using ¾-inch (1.9-cm) exterior-grade plywood. Leave the front entirely open or half open to create a den-like structure for your Siberian.

You can build this type of doghouse inexpensively and clean it easily. Avoid purchasing an expensive doghouse for your Siberian, because he will most likely customize it by chewing the doorway into just the right shape or by making other adjustments to suit his desires.

Construct the house with a flat roof. Siberians enjoy lying on top of their houses and observing their world. Insulate it by providing straw bedding material. It usually is not necessary to heat the doghouse. Place it in a shaded location in the yard or kennel run.

Dog Door

You may consider allowing your Siberian access to a dog door so that he can come in and out of the house freely. Be sure the dog door exits into the dog's kennel run or a securely fenced yard. A dog door that exits into a kennel run with a concrete floor will ensure that a clean and dry Siberian will enter your house, even if your yard is muddy or covered in snow. Do not place the dog door where he will enter into the garage unless you have completely cleared the garage of any safety hazards or materials.

Basic Supplies

Now that you have prepared the outside of your home to offer a comfortable and safe haven to your Siberian Husky, take a moment to address the tools and equipment that will ready the inside of your home for your new family member.

Select a leather or fabric buckle collar sized for your particular dog.

Automobile Safety Restraint

Riding in a crate offers the best protection for your dog while traveling in a car. If your car cannot accommodate a crate, purchase a seatbelt-type restraint made especially for dogs. Not only will a crate or a restraint keep your dog from being thrown around or ejected from the car in the event of an accident, it will confine him until you are ready to release him safely from the car. Never drive with a loose dog inside the car or in the bed of a pickup truck.

Collar

Select a leather or fabric buckle collar sized for your particular puppy or dog. Check his collar often to be sure that he has not outgrown it. (You should be able to run one finger comfortably between a puppy's neck and his collar, and two fingers between an adult dog's neck and his collar.) Choke collars have outlived their usefulness in the world of dog training, given today's more enlightened methods of canine education.

Crate

A crate is one of the most useful tools for raising and managing

A crate is one of the most useful tools for raising and managing a dog.

a dog and is no more cruel than providing a child with her own bedroom. A dog should be able to stand up comfortably in a crate and lie down with room to stretch out. Some large crates come equipped with partitions that you can remove to make the crate smaller to fit a new puppy and then make bigger as he grows into a mature dog. Place the crate in your bedroom. Your dog will benefit from the comfort of your presence, even while you are asleep. Folding crates such as those made by Nylabone have the added value and convenience of being easy to store away when not in use.

Food and Water Bowls

Ceramic bowls are pretty but prone to breakage, while plastic bowls can harbor dangerous bacteria. Tip-proof stainless steel food and water bowls are your best bet because they are unbreakable and easy to clean.

On a related note, be sure that your dog always has access to fresh water both indoors and outdoors.

Identification

- *ID Tags*: Secure identification tags to your dog's collar that display your name, address, and telephone number. If your county has a dog licensing program, obtain a license for him, and attach the tag showing his license number to his collar. In some areas, loose dogs who do not have a license on their collar are considered "abandoned property," and if captured by the animal control department, they may not be given the same consideration as a licensed dog. Attach a rabies vaccination tag to your dog's collar as well so that there will be no question as to whether your dog has been vaccinated in accordance with the law.

- *Tattoos*: Tattooing is a method of permanent identification—unlike an ID tag, which can become lost. By recording the ID number with a registry service, dog owners improve the chances that their lost dog, picked up without collar tags, can be identified and returned to them. The tattoo is usually located on the inside of the dog's thigh or even inside his ear flap. The downside to tattooing is that a dog's heavy coat grows back and can obscure the tattoo. Also, when animal shelter personnel handle a traumatized, loose dog, it may be difficult to search his body for evidence of a tattoo.

- *Microchips*: The advent of microchip identification has revolutionized the permanent identification of dogs. The microchip contains a transponder, antenna, and capacitor, all encased in a tiny glass tube the size of an uncooked grain of rice. A veterinarian implants the chip with an injector that places it under the skin over the top of the dog's shoulders. The process is quick and no more painful than a vaccination. Veterinary offices, shelters, and other pet professionals can use a scanner, waved over the dog's topline, to read the chip. The scanner picks up the ID number from the chip, decodes it, and displays the information on the screen in the scanner.

  Owners register the chip's identification number with a microchip database management service that provides detailed information about the chipped dog and his owner to shelter employees and others who may handle a lost dog.

  Occasionally, a chip will shift out of place, making it

Keeping Your Small Animals Safe

Remember that Siberian Huskies have a strong prey drive. Although they may not want to kill small pets, their rough play may result in an injury to the animal. Keep cats, rabbits, hamsters, birds, and other small pets separated from your Siberian until he has demonstrated complete reliability in their presence.

Choose a leather, nylon, or cotton webbing leash that is appropriate to the size of your dog.

difficult to locate with a scanner. Some manufacturers now produce chips with a polypropylene shell that bonds the chip to the dog's subcutaneous tissue and anchors it in place.

In 1996, one manufacturer introduced a universal scanner that can read all the microchips used by the various identification services, encouraging a wider acceptance of this method of permanent identification.

Indoor Playpen

Many pet stores and pet supply catalogs offer lightweight, portable playpens for puppies, which are also useful for newly acquired older dogs. Unlike a child's playpen, a puppy playpen does not have a floor but instead consists of four plastic grid-like or mesh sides that lock together to form a square enclosure. You can insert additional panels to create an even larger area within the pen. When you place the playpen on a carpeted floor, be sure to put down a protective covering, like an old bed sheet, tarp, or plastic tablecloth. Easy to move around the house, this pen will become your dog's small, beginning world.

Leash

Select a 6-foot (1.8-m) leash appropriate to the size of your puppy or dog. Choose a leather, nylon, or cotton webbing leash, not a metal chain leash, which is hard on the hands. A longer leash of 15 to 20 feet (4.6 to 6.1 m) can be useful for walks in the park. Introduce extendable leashes after you have taught your dog the basics of leash walking.

Toys

For puppies, choose a few toys to use for different purposes. Offer a soft toy for gentle play and as a reward for good behavior.

Offer natural or man-made bones for chewing, as well as balls or throw toys for exercising in the yard. Provide adult dogs with substantial toys for more vigorous play. Nylabone makes some toys that are suitable for Siberian Huskies.

Caring for Your Siberian Husky in Your Absence

Preparing a safe and comfortable environment for your Siberian includes maintaining this environment, even when you are unable to so do yourself. If you work long hours away from home, travel where dogs are not welcome, or just find yourself away from home for a long day, you may want to employ the services of a doggy day care center, a professional pet sitter, or a boarding kennel.

Whatever care option appeals to you and your Siberian, remember that this breed is inquisitive, energetic, welcoming of the company of other dogs, and anxious to be a successful member of a well-functioning pack. Failure to provide an outlet for your Siberian's requirements when you are unavailable to do so will result in boredom, frustration, and the unwanted behaviors that accompany these conditions. There's no need to find yourself contending with these problems with so many useful options at your disposal. Keep in mind that although doggy day care, pet sitters, and boarding kennels provide timely support, they are no

Boarding kennels safely can manage your pet when you are gone for a long period of time.

replacement for your own quality interactions with your Siberian Husky.

Doggy Day Care

Doggy day care centers offer the daytime-only care of pet dogs in a rich environment that includes playtime; supervised interaction with other, well-matched dogs; feeding; and some training services. Although it is a much more humane alternative to leaving your dog alone in your home or a crate for eight to ten hours each weekday, doggy day care cannot replace the guidance and training that your dog needs from you to build a strong relationship. Always stop by the center to make a personal evaluation of the conditions and programs offered before enrolling your Siberian.

Pet Sitters

A professional pet sitter will visit your Siberian in your home.

For dog owners who believe "there's no place like home," professional pet sitters will visit your Siberian in your home on a schedule that you determine. A professional pet sitter offers many

advantages for dogs who do not enjoy rides in the car, who are older or ill, or for owners who just want their dogs surrounded by the familiar sights, sounds, and smells of home. Not only will they feed your dog, walk him, and administer medications, pet sitters will take in your mail and water your plants. For daytime only care, pet sitters may be more convenient than transporting your dog to a day care center far from your home or office. For overnight or extended periods of absence, remember that your dog will be supervised by a pet sitter for only a short time each day and will remain alone overnight.

Boarding Kennels

Although kenneling presents an upsetting alternative for many dogs, boarding kennels safely manage your pet full time during long absences. The adaptable Siberian temperament, along with their ability to get along with other dogs, helps them to handle kenneling. The wide range of services provided by boarding kennels includes housing, grooming, training, selling pet supplies. Some even offer interactive services, such as daily, supervised periods of individual or group play. If you purchased your Siberian from a nearby breeder, check with her about boarding your dog at her kennel. Breeders often will board Siberians from their own stock at their kennel facility for the convenience of their clients.

The excitement is building! Your preparations are complete, and you are ready to add a Siberian Husky to your home. The investment of time and energy to prepare your family and your environment for the arrival of a new dog will pay off in a smoother transition from your dog's first home to his new forever home.

4

FEEDING

Your Siberian Husky

D iet and feeding programs remain some of the most hotly contested topics in the world of canine care and health. Few items of discussion among dog owners, trainers, breeders, veterinarians, and performance-dog handlers generate as much confusion and frustration, in-depth research, or passionate loyalty as the many feeding programs available to the dog owner. As much art as science, properly feeding your Siberian Husky requires you to invest a reasonable amount of thought and energy into creating a program that meets your dog's nutritional needs. Only you can make it happen, because virtually every morsel of food that your dog eats in his entire lifetime originates from you.

Keep in mind that your goal as a dog owner is to identify a feeding program for your Siberian that provides him with the nutrition he needs for optimum health, not just for a minimum state of health that's just a step above malnourishment. You want your Siberian to do more than survive—you want him to thrive.

CREATING A HEALTHY FEEDING PROGRAM

Look to your dog as a collaborator in the process of establishing a healthy feeding program. Be aware of how your dog responds to his food, the condition of his coat, his energy level, and his endurance. Be mindful of your Siberian's natural likes and dislikes for different foods.

Think about your own dietary preferences. You may have difficulty digesting dairy products, feel uncomfortable after eating raw vegetables, or strongly dislike the taste of fish. You will not react enthusiastically when you find these foods on your dinner plate. Although you may eat them if you are really hungry, you will not thrive on them because these foods are not attractive to your particular digestive makeup. In fact, you may become

Look to your dog as a collaborator in the process of establishing a healthy feeding program.

quite unhealthy if all you ever have available to eat is food that is naturally distasteful to you. Your Siberian will express how specific foods appeal to his digestive makeup by his behavior toward these foods, his overall health, and the condition of his stool.

Many people get caught up in trying to copy the food ingredients and feeding regimen of wild canids, like the wolf or the coyote, for their Siberians. Although these animals may represent a part of the ancestry of our domestic canines, many generations of evolution separate wolves and other wild canids from pet dogs—generations in which digestive systems have evolved and changed. Besides, wolves eat rodents, birds, reptiles, insects, and the decomposing organs and flesh of mammals. No owner wants to create a feeding regimen using these ingredients!

The more recent ancestor of the Siberian Husky, the Arctic Chukchi dog, required a relatively small amount of food for his size. Prized by the Chukchi people for his ability to pull loads without requiring a large intake of food, this dog developed a highly efficient metabolism. To brave the extreme cold of the Arctic region, the Chukchi dog ate a diet rich in high-quality, meat-based protein and fat. Also, the diet of the Chukchi dog consisted of a greater quantity of fish than the diets eaten by dogs who developed in a pastoral setting. These factors still influence good feeding practices for the Siberian Husky today.

Creating a feeding program for your Siberian more closely represents a journey than a destination. The options are complex and diverse, and new research, accompanied by the firmly held opinions of respected experts, regularly enters and updates the discussion.

Read labels, do the research, stay current on the findings of reliable sources of study, and consider the behavior and condition of your particular Siberian Husky when deciding on a feeding regimen for him.

TYPES OF DOG FOOD

As mentioned earlier, the diets of ancient dogs consisted mostly of the decaying muscle and organs of their prey. In the last 100 years, domestic dogs ate whatever was left over from the human dinner table, including meat scraps, fish heads, and bones. In

It's Not Agreeable!

Watch for signs that your dog is not tolerating his food very well:

- dull or thin coat
- excessive intestinal gas
- infected ears or ears that produce an overabundance of matter
- itchy patches on the skin or paws
- lack of mealtime enthusiasm or repeated turning away from a particular food
- loose stools
- mucus in the eyes
- patches of hair loss

Strive to provide your dog with a healthy diet that helps his digestive system to thrive.

fact, modern canines have inherited an effective digestive system with a capacity for handling meats and fats and even partially decomposed matter.

A dog's digestive system is shorter and acts more quickly than the human digestive system. It extracts nutrients swiftly and pushes food through quickly, allowing toxins in the food little time to sit in the dog's gut. However, this incredibly efficient canine digestive system has not resulted in the ability to break down the refined carbohydrates, chemical preservatives, and synthetic substances found in most dog food today. As a dog owner, then, you must strive to provide your dog with a healthy diet that helps his digestive system thrive.

Commercial Diets

Each dog food manufacturer creates a unique formula of ingredients and supplements based on its own research, experience, and feeding philosophy. By switching among commercial dog foods in the same category (dry, canned, frozen, etc.) you will expose your dog to a variety of nutritional formulas that will, over time, offer him a more complete array of nutritional elements.

Switching among commercial dog foods in the same category may help to prevent food allergies and improve your dog's digestive capabilities. From a behavior perspective, this method can help to prevent your Siberian from stubbornly refusing all but one brand of dog food. Although each dog food manufacturer would rather have you feed its product exclusively, variety within the same general product category offers significant benefits for your dog.

Remember to switch among high-quality commercial dog foods, and introduce the new food gradually into your dog's diet. A gradual change encourages your dog's intestinal bacteria to adjust to the new food without causing gas or diarrhea. Switch dog foods only every two to four months, then stick with the new food and switch again in another two to four months.

Dry Food

Originally created as a "convenience food," dry dog food (also known as kibble) has become, for many dogs, the only food they will ever eat. In today's busy households, the equivalent of canine fast food represents the major, if not only, source of nutrition for a dog.

All dry food manufacturers add a vitamin and mineral premix to their basic food formula to ensure that the final product contains at least the minimum amounts of these nutrients, as determined by the Association of American Feed Control Officials (AAFCO)

Label Language

When selecting a commercially prepared dog food, carefully read the ingredient labels to find the best quality food for your Siberian Husky. Follow the guidelines listed below:

- Look for a product's "guaranteed analysis."
- Look for two or more animal-protein sources (species-specific meat or meat meal or fish), once as the first ingredient on the label and again among the first five ingredients.
- Avoid meat or poultry by-products.
- Avoid nonspecies-specific protein or fat sources ("meat meal" or "animal fat").
- Avoid artificial colors, flavors, sweeteners, or chemical preservatives.
- Look for whole grains and vegetables. Avoid soy, which is difficult for Siberians to digest.
- Look for broth used instead of water in the formula.
- Check the product date codes.

for certain diets. (The AAFCO describes different diet profiles, such as maintenance, growth, senior, performance, or lactation, to address the needs of specific types of dogs and specific stages in a dog's life.) Manufacturers use the premix because the process of cooking the ingredients to make kibble, whether it's baked or extruded, and then forming it into pellets, destroys many of the vitamins and minerals in the original ingredients of the food. These premixes are added to a base formula whose quality differs widely among manufacturers. Some manufacturers design their base formulas to meet the minimum AAFCO standards and use all sorts of low-cost by-products of the human food or animal-feed manufacturing industry. These ingredients may include chicken feet, brewers rice (small fragments of rice created during the rice milling process), and corn gluten meal (the dried by-product of the corn syrup manufacturing process). To make the final product more palatable to the dog (and to the owner's senses) and to increase the shelf life of the final product, these manufacturers add artificial colors, flavors, sweeteners, and chemical preservatives. "Generic" and low-cost dry dog food brands result from this type of formulation.

Dry food is a convenient option for many dog owners.

Higher quality and higher cost dry dog foods also start with a vitamin and mineral premix, but the basic formula contains whole foods from reliable sources. These whole foods may include animal protein in the form of meat (identified by species, such as "chicken" or "lamb"), meat meal (dehydrated meat), whole vegetables, and whole grains. These manufacturers purchase more expensive raw ingredients from meat processing companies that guarantee the health of the feed animals and the freshness of the meat. They develop ongoing relationships with reputable growers of vegetables and grains. Some use organic ingredients in their formulas, and they may use natural substances, like vitamins C and E, to preserve the product.

Dry dog food must absorb moisture before a dog's digestive enzymes can break the food down. It either absorbs moisture from the dog's digestive tract, creating an imbalance there, or the dog feels the need to gulp water after eating the dry food. The added water causes the dry food to expand in the stomach, triggering an uncomfortable, bloated feeling in the dog. The dog may become restless and resort to chewing his paws or legs an hour or two after eating.

If you feed dry dog food to your Siberian, place the food in his bowl and add 1½ to 2 cups (354.9 to 473.2 ml) of water to the food. Let it sit on your kitchen countertop for about an hour or until the food has soaked up most of the water. Leave any remaining liquid in the bowl, which may contain important nutrients that leached out of the food while it soaked, and serve the liquid as a "gravy."

Always check the "sell by" information on all dry dog food labels, especially those preserved with vitamins C and E instead of chemicals. These foods have a shorter shelf life than chemically preserved dog foods.

Canned Food

Although slightly less convenient than dry dog food, canned dog food offers many nutritional advantages. Canned dog food usually contains much more meat, an important source of protein, than does dry dog food. A mixture of more than about 50 percent meat literally gums up the machinery used to manufacture dry dog food. Canned dog food may contain up to 95 percent meat. That fact may explain why dogs really like canned food, even though it's smelly to humans—it contains lots of meat!

Moist ingredients, like fish, eggs, fresh vegetables, and whole, cooked grains, present no problem for use in canned dog foods and do not have to be dehydrated in the manufacturing process. Therefore, they abound in canned dog foods. Canned dog food manufacturers also add a vitamin and mineral premix to the food to ensure that at least the minimum amounts of these nutrients enter the final product. Canned dog food contains about 75 to 80 percent moisture, which helps the food mixture pass through the mixing and filling machines during the manufacturing process. This moisture in the food precludes the need to rob moisture from the dog's digestive system to break down the food and keeps him from craving water during and after mealtime.

The canning process has virtually no effect on the protein, fat, and vitamin content of the source ingredients of the food. (Vegetables left in the refrigerator for a week or more can lose vitamins faster than canned vegetables.) Preservatives are not required in canned dog food, which has an extended shelf life based on its oxygen-free environment. And because the source ingredients of canned dog food most closely resemble materials that are naturally the most desirable and digestible for dogs, manufacturers use fewer, if any, artificial means of enhancing palatability, such as sweeteners and flavorings.

The quality of canned dog food varies according to the quality of the source ingredients used to make the food. As in dry dog foods, look for whole meats (identified by species) or fish, and seek out whole grains and vegetables in the ingredients list. Select canned foods that use meat, poultry, or fish broth in place of water to provide the desired moisture content of the food. Also, look for manufacturers that use organic ingredients in their products. Expect to pay more for canned dog foods that utilize high-quality source ingredients.

Canned dog food must be refrigerated once opened, and it should be consumed within a day or two after opening.

Semi-Moist Food

Semi-moist dog food is soft tidbits of food packaged in serving-size pouches. The makers often add a gravy-type substance to the food. However, convenience is the only claim to fame for this type of dog food, and it's a slim claim at best. Manufacturers of semi-moist food generally use low-quality protein sources, like meat

Storage

Keep fresh dog food and opened canned dog food refrigerated. Store dry dog food in its original bag, and place the bag in a container that seals tightly. Store the container in a cool, dry place—but not in the garage. Heat and oxygen are the enemies of dog food.

If you empty dry dog food directly into a plastic container, use FDA-approved food-grade plastic containers. Metal containers can affect the taste of food. Nonfood-grade plastic containers can interact with the food and leach out vitamins. How do you know if the plastic is really food grade? If you place tomato sauce or pureed fresh carrots in the plastic container, and the food stains the container, leaving a residue even after you wash it, the plastic is not food-grade material.

by-products or meat meal. Semi-moist dog foods contain artificial colors, flavors, and preservatives, as well as added sweeteners. These ingredients provide no nutritional value; their function is to make the food more appealing to dogs and their owners. A high-quality canned dog food is just as convenient as a semi-moist dog food, and it offers more nutrition with less fillers.

Prepared Meal Bases

Meal bases are a relatively new entrant into the commercial dog food market, most of which require the addition of fresh meat, either raw or cooked, to complete the meal. These products help dog owners who are trying to prepare a complete and balanced diet for their dogs using fresh, quality ingredients but who do not want to prepare an entirely homemade dog food. The high cost of these meal bases reflects their convenience and quality ingredients.

Most meal bases consist of grains and vegetables in a dehydrated state. The owner adds water to rehydrate the ingredients and includes fresh meat to the base to complete the meal. Some manufacturers intend that dog owners cook their meal bases along with the meat. Others request that owners add an oil supplement, like flaxseed oil, to the meal. Almost all these products make no claim to meet AAFCO standards because they are not complete meals when eaten without the meat added by the owner.

Many of these products contain herbs, nutritional supplements like bee pollen, and added vitamins and minerals.

Special Canine Diets

Commercial dog foods labeled "competition," "performance," "active," or "high stress" usually contain the highest levels of protein, fat, and calories. Some of the formulas may provide as much as half the calories as fat. It takes a really active dog to eat a food like that and still remain lean and trim.

Manufacturers have targeted the small niche food market as a way to attract owners to their commercial dog foods. A few manufacturers are using their performance formulas to draw finicky eaters to their food line because dogs find the high protein and high fat levels of these formulas very attractive.

Breed-specific diets represent another way that manufacturers are creating and filling small niche markets in the dog food industry. With origins in the theory that certain breeds thrive

Pure Water

When putting together a healthy feeding regimen for your Siberian, don't forget to make pure drinking water available to him. Long-term exposure to chlorine and other purifying agents in tap water may be harmful to dogs.

Water purifies, detoxifies, and lubricates the body, and it must be "empty" of toxins and dissolved impurities to do its job of capturing and carrying these substances out of a dog's system. Steam-distilled water is the purest drinking water and efficiently captures and flushes waste material from the body.

on certain food formulas based on the geographic origins of the breed, suppliers offer specialty, breed-specific foods, like rice-based formulas for Asian breeds.

These manufacturers also produce high-protein, high-fat, and fish-based formulas for northern breeds. However, a wholesome diet is particular to an individual dog more than to a breed. A moderately active Siberian Husky does not require the high protein and high fat contained in a "northern breed diet." There's no substitute for tailoring a diet to your particular Siberian with the help of a canine nutritionist or veterinarian.

NONCOMMERCIAL DIETS

Today's dog owners have come to appreciate the value of feeding the most natural, high-quality diet possible to their dogs. They reap the rewards of owning dogs who live long, healthy, athletic lives. Many owners have embraced the minimally processed, frozen raw diets available on the market or have taken on the task of preparing a homemade diet for their dogs using fresh, natural ingredients.

Frozen Raw Food

Dr. Ian Billinghurst brought the now well-known BARF diet to the forefront of canine nutrition. The acronym BARF originally stood for the Bones and Raw Food diet but later was polished up and referred to as the Biologically Appropriate Raw Food diet. The terms are used interchangeably, along with other common descriptions, such as the evolutionary diet, the natural diet, and the species-appropriate diet.

Minced bones; human-grade beef, chicken, turkey, lamb, muscle and organ meat; vegetables; fruit; herbs; and supplements compose the basic ingredients of the BARF diet. Dr. Billinghurst's canine diet formula contains no grains because he believes that dogs do not require carbohydrates in their diets.

At first, Dr. Billinghurst and other BARF diet proponents anticipated that owners would create their dogs' meals, according to the BARF precepts, at home from original source ingredients. They instructed owners how to combine the meat, vegetables, and bones into a complete meal mix. However, several manufacturers now offer commercially prepared, frozen, meat-based versions of this diet for dog owners concerned about getting the diet formula

Provide your Siberian with plenty of fresh, cool water.

just right or about handling raw meat safely.

Pet and health food stores across the country have begun to carry frozen, raw canine diets in their freezers, but most owners have to order the food for home delivery. Manufacturers adhere to differing philosophies about the contents of the food and packaging methods. If an order will sit on your front porch for a few hours before someone can place it in the freezer, carefully consider packaging and delivery options when ordering a commercial raw food diet.

Because of the high cost of these diets, many owners mix them with dry or canned dog foods. However, the goal of the BARF diet is to completely eliminate cooked or processed foods of any kind from a dog's diet and replace them with whole, raw foods.

Some manufacturers guarantee their BARF frozen meals to be complete and balanced. Others sell meal-based mixes and instruct the owner to select and add supplements to satisfy their dog's particular nutritional needs.

Homemade Food

Recipes for homemade dog food fill the pages of many books about canine nutrition. The complexity of some of the formulas, especially those that include a parade of ingredients like apple cider vinegar, cod liver oil, kelp, and cooked eggs in the shell, cause many dog owners to shake their heads, shrug, and return to an evaluation of commercial dog foods.

However, easy-to-make and convenient-to-feed homemade diet recipes exist for the dog owner willing to take the plunge and make a commitment to preparing a homemade, wholesome dog food for her Siberian. Consult the "Basic Recipe for Homemade Dog Food" sidebar in this chapter for an example of a simple, easy to prepare, fresh-food canine diet.

A properly prepared and well-balanced homemade diet will provide all the members of your canine family with the nutrition that they need for optimum health.

SUPPLEMENTS

Choices in commercially prepared dog foods pale in comparison to the choices available in dietary supplements for dogs. Aside from individual vitamin and mineral additives, owners can choose from multivitamin and mineral mixes formulated for a dog's various life stages and activity levels. Supplements address coat condition, skin care, medical conditions, structural problems, energy boosts, and even sports hydration for the performance dog. Indeed, supplements have a respectable place in the canine diet if selected and used judiciously. The decision to supplement your Siberian's diet should be a collaborative effort between you, your dog, and your canine health care team.

Keep in mind that a properly fed dog requires minimal supplementation to maintain vibrant good health. Use common sense, and don't subscribe to every new fad in canine diet supplementation. Let your own research, advice from your conventional and holistic veterinarians, and your dog act as your guides.

Vitamins and Minerals

For a healthy dog, keep supplementation simple and conservative in dosage amounts. Overdosing with vitamin and mineral supplements can cause as much harm as nutrient deficiencies. Be especially careful of overdosing with the fat-soluble vitamins like E, A, and K. A dog's body retains these vitamins in his fatty tissue, and too much of a good thing can lead to vitamin toxicity. Your veterinarian or canine nutritionist is the best person to help you select an all-purpose vitamin and mineral supplement for your particular Siberian's needs.

Enzymes

If you feed only one other dietary supplement beyond a multivitamin and mineral supplement, choose a balanced digestive enzyme product made especially for dogs. Many holistic veterinarians agree that if you added nothing else to a commercial or homemade canine diet except digestive enzymes, you'll witness an overall improvement in your dog's health.

Found in all cells and fluids in the dog's body, enzymes create and speed up chemical reactions. Digestive enzymes are the catalysts of the digestive process and a vital element for accomplishing proper digestion and consumption of

Basic Recipe for Homemade Dog Food

Volume Proportions:

Animal protein and fat source: about 50%

Vegetable source: about 25%

Grain source: about 25%

Bone meal: ¾ to 1 tablespoon (11.1 to 14.8 ml) per pound (0.5 kg) of meat

Sources (Human Consumption Grade or Organic):

Animal protein and fat: beef, chicken, turkey, fish, deer, and eggs; occasionally include organ meat (beef liver, beef kidney, chicken gizzards, etc.)

Vegetables: carrots, zucchini, celery, yams, peas, etc. (No onions, please! Onions are toxic to dogs.)

Grains: rolled oats, brown rice, millet, barley, quinoa, etc.

Supplements: bone meal (mandatory), others as determined by owners and a veterinary nutritionist

Preparation:

Meat: raw or lightly cooked, cut into chewable chunks, or ground

Vegetables: raw or lightly steamed, pureed in a blender or food processor using water as needed

Grains: cooked longer than required for human consumption and with extra water so that the end product is a bit mushy

Making It Easy:

Puree a few cups (ml) of vegetables and cook a few cups (ml) of grains and refrigerate them in storage containers for use during the next few days. Freeze large quantities of ground meats in patties to defrost each day, or freeze batches of lightly cooked or raw meat chunks in small containers for individual use.

nutrients. An array of appropriate enzymes plays a critical role in the efficient utilization of your Siberian's food and may make the difference between vibrant good health and disease.

TREATS

After you have devoted a considerable amount of time to working out a healthy feeding regimen for your Siberian, don't undermine it by using treats and training rewards full of additives, fillers, and other chemicals. However, trainers suggest that owners offer "high-value" treats or rewards during training sessions. "High-value" treats usually mean those smelly, yummy tidbits that motivate your dog to work hard and find out exactly what you want him to do to earn those delicious morsels. Unfortunately, those kinds of treats contain high levels of fat, sweeteners, and other ingredients that you have worked diligently to minimize in his diet.

Thankfully, many manufacturers produce "healthy" treats created with whole-food ingredients and natural sweeteners, like honey and molasses. Read labels, and avoid treats containing artificial preservatives, artificial colors, and propylene glycol (a chemical used to keep foods containing meat moist, chewy, and colorful for an extended time). Don't become too concerned about the presence of natural sweeteners or natural flavor enhancers in your dog's treats. Treats don't have to rigidly conform to the characteristics of a superior dog food formula. Just don't offer treats that contain the potentially harmful substances that you have diligently avoided in other areas of your Siberian's life.

Feed your Siberian healthy, high-value treats during training sessions.

Search your refrigerator and pantry for string cheese, bits of leftover meat, and even organic, O-shaped breakfast cereal. Collect a couple of easy recipes for making homemade treats, which are a big hit because the ingredient lists for these recipes usually include things like garlic, canned tuna, applesauce, and other foods that dogs really enjoy.

Feed your Siberian small treats, and when you are in the midst of an intense training schedule, carefully reduce the volume of his meals to account for his increased intake of treats.

FEEDING FOR EVERY LIFE STAGE

Your Siberian Husky looks forward to mealtime, just like you do! He deserves to enjoy a moment of undisturbed calm and quiet when he eats. Feed your Siberian where the close presence of other dogs will not crowd him, children will not interrupt him, and you will not find him otherwise underfoot. Resist the advice of some trainers to feed your dog by portioning out your Siberian's meal as rewards during a training session. There's more to life than training sessions—namely, a good, quiet dinner!

Feeding the Puppy

Growing puppies require higher levels of energy provided by food with high protein levels from quality sources, as well as a moderate amount of fat. Most commercial puppy foods contain 25 to 28 percent protein, and the fat content in puppy food ranges from about 12 to 18 percent. Puppies require adequate amounts of fat for growth, so stay away from any reduced-fat or "light" puppy foods.

If possible, bring home a small amount of the puppy food fed by your Siberian's breeder. Continue to feed the breeder's food while your puppy adjusts to his new environment, and use it to gradually acclimate your puppy to the food that you will give him in the future. Ask your breeder to provide you with a diet sheet describing the food and feeding schedule that she recommends for her puppies.

Feed a puppy three to four times a day until he is finished teething, which is at about six to eight months old. Allow the puppy to consume all he wants in 10 to 15 minutes, then remove the food. Puppies and young dogs go through growth spurts, so keep a close eye on your pup to be certain that he maintains a good weight.

System Detoxification

Don't become concerned if your dog occasionally skips a meal, has a short bout of diarrhea, or vomits after eating a meal. Dogs naturally detoxify their systems in this way. However, these events should be relatively rare and should not include bloody stools or fever. Ask your veterinarian to examine your Siberian if these conditions continue.

Feed an adult Siberian Husky twice a day.

A lean puppy is healthier than a fat puppy. Overweight puppies may develop structural problems because their body weight has put too much stress on growing bones.

Feeding the Adult

Adult maintenance formulas generally offer protein in a wide range, from about 20 to 30 percent. Most adult dog foods contain a higher fat level than the AAFCO suggests for an adult maintenance food profile, ranging from 6 percent to 20 percent. Fat increases the palatability of dog food, so manufacturers use it to lure and keep enthusiastic canine consumers. On the other hand, extremely low-fat foods result in poor coat condition and flaky skin. Because the Siberian Husky must receive optimum nutrition from a small amount of food, do not feed very low-fat and low-protein diets unless your veterinarian recommends it.

Feed an adult dog twice a day. Some owners eventually transition to feeding once a day, pointing to the fact that days may pass between meals for wolves and dogs in the wild. However, wolves gorge their meals in the wild and have developed a metabolism that handles their cycles of feast and famine. Two meals a day of commercial food or a homemade diet helps your dog to stay satisfied and avoid feelings of hunger and food-related anxiety. A dog not worried about his next meal will focus more attention on training sessions and have ready access to energy sources for his long-term endurance needs.

Feeding the Senior

Dogs of different sizes and breeds age at different rates. Small dogs enjoy the longest average life spans, while large and giant breeds have the shortest life spans. A veterinarian may suggest that a giant-breed dog who engages in a low or moderate amount of exercise switch to a senior food as early as five years old. Small and highly active dogs may continue to eat a performance diet until they reach ten years of age. The older, medium-size Siberian Husky requires a nutrient-rich food if he eats small quantities at mealtime. However, let your dog's physique, activity level, and the advice of your veterinarian guide you about when to introduce senior-formula commercial foods into his diet.

Most commercial senior dog diets compare with the manufacturer's "light" or weight-loss formulas for adult dogs. Because dogs tend to gain weight as they age, manufacturers provide fewer calories and less protein and fat in their senior diets, making them almost interchangeable with their weight-loss formulas. A lower level of dietary protein goes easier on an older canine's kidneys. However, if an older dog remains very active, a senior diet will not provide the nutrition he requires to stay in peak condition.

FOOD PROBLEMS

Don't allow dinnertime to become a source of bad habits or problem behaviors in your Siberian. A good meal eaten in a quiet place and at the dog's own speed should be an enjoyable part of your Siberian's day.

Be mindful of portion control when feeding your Siberian, because an overweight dog is an unhealthy dog. Also, encourage proper manners in your Siberian at dinnertime so that he will learn to enjoy this time without clashing with you in the process.

Cravings

Does your Siberian turn away from chicken but steal a hamburger every chance he gets? Does he eat heartily when you add eggs to his dinner but pick all around the cottage cheese? Chicken may upset your dog's stomach, and he may have an allergy to dairy products. He also may need more vitamin K in his diet, which is abundant in eggs.

If your Siberian Husky demonstrates a marked preference for certain foods, chances are that he needs those foods for a balanced diet or that those foods naturally agree with his digestive chemistry. Honor his needs and modify your feeding plan accordingly.

Obesity

The list of health risks associated with canine obesity continues to grow. Studies trace a number of canine musculoskeletal problems, including osteoarthritis, to obesity. Excess weight complicates medical and surgical procedures and may delay healing. An overweight dog may even contract diabetes and have difficulty fighting infections.

Is Your Siberian Overweight?

Weight charts are helpful and offer a starting point for determining the best weight for your dog, but a visual and hands-on approach is the best method of assessing canine body weight. Here's how to do it:

1. Look down on your Siberian from directly above. A trim dog's body narrows behind the ribcage and in front of the hips. You can see a clearly defined waist, sometimes called an "hourglass" shape. If he lacks the hourglass shape, he may be carrying excess weight. If his waist appears rounded outward, he may be obese.

2. Look at your dog from the side while he's standing. His stomach should tuck up behind his ribcage and in front of his hips. If his abdomen is not clearly defined, he may be overweight.

3. Can you feel your Siberian's ribcage easily through a thin layer of flesh? Run your fingers along his side toward his tail. If you can't feel his ribs along the way, a layer of fat probably covers his ribs. If you can feel fleshy deposits on the dog's body, especially on the spine and base of the tail, your dog may be obese.

How to Help Your Dog Lose Weight

Although overeating and lack of exercise are the usual culprits in overweight dogs, several medical conditions can play a role in putting the excess pounds (kg) onto your dog's frame. Structural conditions like hip dysplasia, osteoarthritis, and sports injuries to ligaments, muscles, and joints can limit your dog's activity level and contribute to weight gain. Metabolic diseases like diabetes also can cause obesity. Consult with your veterinarian before you become convinced that your Siberian needs the help of a serious weight-loss plan.

If, however, your Siberian simply takes in more calories than he burns, you must address the source of the problem before your dog develops the health problems associated with obesity. Here are your weight-loss options:

- Slowly reduce the total amount of food that you give your dog, or change to a diet lower in calories and fat. Remember, your dog didn't add the excess weight overnight. Removing the weight safely also takes time. Rapid weight loss can disturb the proper functioning of your dog's metabolic system and cause a loss of muscle tissue as well as fat, which works against the weight-loss program itself. Don't attempt to take off more than 2 percent of your dog's body weight in a week. Strive to reduce his body weight about 10 percent over the course of several weeks, then check his weight and perform the visual and hands-on test again. Reassess your weight-loss goals for your dog, and modify his weight-loss plan accordingly. Be sure that he continues to eat enough food to stay healthy.

- Increase your dog's exercise level to burn off the excess weight. Don't rely on him to exercise himself in the backyard. Play with him, walk him, and participate in high-energy sports activities, like agility or sledding. Find a place where your dog can swim.

- Eliminate opportunities for your dog to scavenge for extra food in the garbage, food bowls of other pets, and compost piles.

- Use treats mindfully as a reward for demonstrating specific behavior in a training moment, not for just looking cute. Don't fall victim to the behaviors that your dog adopts to

"train" you to feed him treats. Does he stand in front of the pantry or treat jar and look at you with soulful eyes? Does he beg and drool while you eat, waiting for the moment when you will hand over the scraps on your dinner plate? In addition to becoming a nuisance, your dog has trained you to help him pack on the weight.

- Reduce stress in your dog's life. Many dogs respond to stress by eating anything and everything they can find. Find ways to release his pent-up energy, improve your relationship with him through training and play, and be sure that his environment is comfortable and clean.

- Do not "free-feed" your dog. Owners who free-feed keep food in their dog's food bowl at all times, thinking that the dog, being a creature with a natural sensibility about eating, will self-regulate his own food intake. However, the rigors of a dog's contemporary lifestyle and the abundant availability of food to most companion dogs have redefined food consumption as a stress reliever, an opportunity to exert some control over his own environment, and a source of entertainment. Owners must remain vigilant about regulating a dog's food intake and weight. Allow your dog 10 to 15 minutes to eat what you serve him at every meal, then remove his bowl until the next feeding time.

Plan to manage your dog's weight for the rest of his life. Perform the hands-on test regularly. Weigh your dog once a month, and immediately take steps to control weight gain in its early stages.

Food Bowl Guarding

Overexcitement and aggression associated with mealtime in general—and the food bowl in particular—represent one of the worst lapses in canine manners. Some dogs come close to knocking their owners to the ground when they arrive with food bowl in hand. Others snarl, growl, or even bite when someone approaches their food bowl while they are eating. Not only are these behaviors an inconvenience, they are dangerous to owners, children, and other pets in the home.

From the first, teach your dog to allow you to remove his food bowl, even while he is eating from it. To do so, prepare his meal and have a really special treat, like cheese or liver treats, handy. Place the food bowl down. When your dog just begins to eat, gently

Your Siberian needs exercise to help him maintain a healthy weight.

approach his bowl and say his name. When he looks up, praise him and give him the special treat from your hand. At the next meal, approach his bowl and gently touch the rim. If he calmly accepts your actions, praise him and give him a special treat from your hand. At the next meal, pick up his food bowl. When he accepts your action, praise him and give him the special treat from your hand and add a few treats to his food bowl on top of his dinner. At the next mealtime, approach his bowl and just toss some goodies like healthy table scraps into his bowl. He will learn that when he allows you to approach and even take his food bowl, he will receive treats that are even better than the dinner itself.

Do not annoy your dog with this training. If he performs correctly, you have made your point quickly and can just reinforce the behavior once in a while. Do not work on exchanging access to the food bowl for treats every day, and only perform the exercise once per meal. However, it's a good idea to continue to ask your dog to sit or stand quietly every time that you offer him his dinner.

These activities do not conflict with the "don't use his dinner for training" rule. First, you are specifically training behaviors that center on dinnertime manners. Second, after your Siberian learns dinnertime manners to your satisfaction, you will cease to require that he perform the full complement of behaviors each and every time you feed him.

As a result of this training, your dog will approach dinner with some decorum, which is the ultimate goal of the training. Every few weeks, you may wish to reinforce his good manners by asking for access to his food bowl during dinner in exchange for a goodie, but your aim to achieve proper dinnertime manners in your dog will have been met.

If your dog is already guarding his food bowl, here are a few things that you can do to solve the problem:

- From the first day that your Siberian enters your home, train him to wait patiently for his dinner and to allow you to have access to his food bowl, even while he eats.
- When you carry a bowl of food to your Siberian, do not give it to him unless he remains calm. Decide on the behavior you want from your dog at mealtime, and insist that he offer it before he receives his meal.
- For a puppy, wait with the bowl in your hand until he is calm. Because he doesn't recognize commands like *sit* and *wait* just yet, rely on his natural behaviors for now. Because he will have to look up at you while you are holding his bowl, he will most likely sit. The moment his rear end hits the floor or he calmly stands still, smile, say "Good puppy," and gently place the bowl down. Repeat these steps at each dinnertime, and you will have a pup who parks his rear end on the floor rather quickly.
- For a dog whose education includes the lessons *sit* and *stay* or *wait*, use these commands when presenting his dinner.

If your dog has developed aggressive habits associated with his meals, consult a trainer who specializes in aggressive-behavior modification. Jumping into a food-bowl training session with an already aggressive food-bowl guarder can be unpleasant, if not dangerous.

Begging, Drooling, and Whining

Positive reinforcement drives repetitive behavior, good or bad. This concept applies to dogs who beg for food and develop all sorts of other bad habits, like drooling and standing watch by the dog cookie jar. In addition to being unattractive, these habits, alone and

General Feeding Considerations

Always consult with a veterinarian, a holistic veterinary practitioner, or a veterinary nutritionist about your Siberian's diet, especially when feeding a performance dog, a highly stressed dog, a sick dog, or a pregnant dog.

From the beginning, train your dog to wait patiently for his dinner and to allow you to have access to his food bowl.

certainly when coupled with other irritating behaviors, undermine the good relationship that you want to enjoy with your Siberian. They lead to banishments from the dining room, seclusion when company arrives, and a general sense of having a dog always underfoot and searching for tidbits rather than enjoying the pleasure of your company.

The solution is clear but requires unflagging determination on your part:

- Never feed your dog from the table, your favorite chair where you snack, the kitchen countertop, or any other place where you do not want your dog to ever expect a handout.
- Never treat your dog from his cookie jar on his command. Dispense treats when it's your idea to do so and mostly as a reward for good behavior.
- Stop any inappropriate feeding practices that you have already started. (Be strong!)

Your serious attention to developing good feeding habits will aid you in your quest to provide your Siberian with a lifetime of good health.

Chapter

5

GROOMING
Your Siberian Husky

O
riginally, dog breeders strived to produce dogs whose
coats assisted and supported their animals in the work
that they were bred to do. For example, the curly coat of
the Poodle protects this water-retrieving breed from cold
temperatures, keeping his joints warm and comfortable
while serving as a shield against briars and undergrowth
in the field. The hard, flat, straight outer "jacket" of the
Border Terrier allows these dogs to slip through the
underground tunnels where rodents and other "vermin"
reside, as they bolt these animals out of hiding for the
hunter to dispatch. Their slick coats shed mud and dirt, and
their undercoats retain body heat.

Today, many of the AKC-recognized dog breeds
sport coats that have become extravagant and
exaggerated, especially during the more recent
generations of human-directed breeding.
Although dogs groom their own coats with
their tongues, paws, and teeth, these
overstated coats create a significant
challenge for the dog's self-grooming tools
and require diligent upkeep from his
owner. The cottony-soft coat of the Soft-
Coated Wheaten Terrier mats quickly
and demands daily combing. The
complex cording of the Puli coat
needs careful management,
or his coat will experience a
buildup of mats, knots, dirt,
stickers, seeds, and other

The Siberian Husky's coat requires only a minimal amount of care to look stunningly beautiful.

irritants that may lead to skin eruptions, eye and ear problems, and other health conditions.

In contrast, the Siberian Husky has retained his original, naturally functional coat, which requires a minimal amount of care from his owner to look stunningly beautiful. The owner of a Siberian has no need to collect an impressive array of clippers, strippers, dematting tools, specialty shears, and other elaborate grooming equipment. Your relatively small investment of time spent in caring for your Siberian Husky's coat and other grooming needs will result in a lovely animal whose handsome appearance reflects overall good health.

GROOMING FROM THE SIBERIAN POINT OF VIEW

Nobody bathed wild canids or cleaned their ears or trimmed their nails, and they seemed to get along just fine. So why groom a "natural" breed like the Siberian Husky?

In the wild, an animal moves freely from place to place and can leave an area that has become infested with a colony of fleas, ticks, intestinal worms, or other parasites. Domestic animals, on the other hand, live in the same quarters for years, and the eggs and larvae of parasites may continually reinfest their environment. Proper grooming removes these parasites and their eggs from the dog, and proper kennel management removes them from the dog's environment. The domestic surroundings of the contemporary Siberian differ significantly from the Arctic habitat of his ancestors. The dust, dirt, and debris that collect in your Siberian's fur contain a variety of toxins and contaminants that range from lint produced by synthetic fibers, to brake dust from automobiles, to lawn-maintenance chemicals. Removing this debris from your Siberian's coat is preferable to allowing him to clean himself and swallow this material.

In addition, regular grooming encourages the skin's natural toxin elimination process by stimulating the production of secretions that clear toxins from the dog's body. Brushing removes these secretions and contributes to the continuation of the detoxification cycle.

But one of the most important benefits of grooming your Siberian Husky is the opportunity to closely interact with your dog, one on one. Use grooming sessions to train him to willingly accept hands-on care from you and to prepare him for veterinary scrutiny and treatment. A grooming session also presents the opportunity to check the state of your dog's

Don't Touch!

The first attempts to groom a dog who has been treated roughly, who has been improperly socialized, or who has been chronically ill in the past requires patience and lots of understanding. Gentle grooming helps such dogs learn to tolerate and even look forward to human touch.

When a dog who has always enjoyed being groomed and touched suddenly resists these things, consult your veterinarian. This change may indicate an injury or illness that is causing pain. Use the grooming session to check for any negative reactions to touch from your dog, and act accordingly:

- *Avoidance body language*: retreating, cowering, avoiding eye contact, licking, yawning, ducking the head, flattening the ears, urinating
- *Confrontational body language*: raising hackles, staring, lunging, growling, snapping, showing the whites of the eyes
- *Stress-indicating body language*: tensing, freezing, moving away, pupil dilation, panting, increased heart rate

Grooming provides an intense bonding experience with your dog.

health and enables you to identify a problem before it blossoms into a full-fledged emergency.

As a bonding experience, grooming familiarizes your dog with your touch, tones of voice, and expectations regarding his behavior. Touch is an important way for social beings to connect with one another. Dogs and humans are both social species, and humans have developed and encouraged their dogs' social dependency on them. Therefore, a dog's need for touch is strong.

Many animal studies have found that petting and other pleasant touching reduces a dog's heart rate and blood pressure in stressful or painful situations. Others report that animals who were repeatedly touched demonstrated more resistance to stress, disease, and the effects of aging. Touching enhances the development of the brain and nervous system and can mediate behavioral responses in dogs.

Take advantage of the many benefits that grooming presents to keep your Siberian's appearance in tip-top shape, monitor and manage his overall health, and build a strong bond with him through the magic of gentle touch.

THE GROOMING EXPERIENCE

Grooming your Siberian starts the moment that the intention to groom him enters your mind, not the moment you put comb to coat. How you indicate to your dog that you are about to groom him and how you manage the preparations for a grooming session make all the difference between an annoying struggle and a bonding experience enjoyed by you and your dog.

Dogs expertly read human body language and other subconscious indicators, like tone of voice or speed of movement. With this in mind, use your Siberian's attention to your behavior to announce that a pleasant grooming session is about to unfold. Approach him quietly, and literally tell him that you plan to take some time to pretty him up and check him out. He will not understand your language, but he will discern a world of information from your attitude and tone of voice. As you speak to him, your body and voice communicate your intentions and provide fair warning of events to follow. After all, not many people would take kindly to being pulled suddenly from their favorite chair and hustled into the shower without a word of warning! Don't ask your dog to tolerate the equivalent of such treatment.

Move slowly, speak quietly, and pet your dog for a minute or two before you begin the grooming session. Ask him to do a quick trick for a treat to transition him into a cooperative frame of mind.

Place your Siberian on a grooming table with a nonskid surface. The table clearly defines the boundaries of his area while you are grooming him and discourages him from struggling during the session. Also, using a grooming table helps your Siberian to understand the difference between a grooming session, which requires him to observe certain rules of behavior, and a play session on the floor, in which the rules are entirely different!

When to Begin Grooming

Begin grooming your Siberian as soon as he joins your family. Puppies who have been handled gently and taught good behavior on the grooming table remain a pleasure to groom throughout their lives. Also, ask your Siberian's breeder to demonstrate proper grooming techniques for your dog. If you attend conformation dog shows, stroll around the crating and preparation area and observe the professional staff grooming the Siberians entered in the show.

Keep a stash of treats handy. Hand them out to your dog for maintaining proper decorum on the grooming table, such as calmly accepting brushing, nail trimming, ear cleaning, and a thorough, overall examination. Tell him repeatedly how well he is behaving as you groom him.

Don't overdo any one grooming session. Take regular breaks for a quick trip outdoors or a short, calm play session. Getting his teeth cleaned, coat brushed, nails clipped, and ears cleaned in one session asks too much from a dog and casts an unpleasant and stressful aura over the grooming process in general.

After completing the grooming session, let your Siberian remain on the table for a minute so that he doesn't pick up the habit of trying to jump off the table the moment you lay down the brush. Smile and tell him how handsome he looks. When he's back on the floor, pet him and tell him how much you enjoy seeing him look so lovely.

COAT MAINTENANCE

When a Siberian Husky sheds his undercoat, you instantly develop a close relationship with your vacuum cleaner. Twice a year, Siberians "blow" out their undercoats, releasing a profuse amount of hair. This intense shedding period lasts for three weeks or more and creates a blizzard of dog hair in your home and on your clothes, even when you take the time to vacuum continually and brush your Siberian daily. This shedding schedule can be climate-dependent. Some dogs who live in very warm areas of the country that lack clearly defined seasonal changes may shed year round.

Some Siberians shed their undercoats all at once; others shed in uneven clumps, starting on the legs and thighs. Shedding then progresses to the body and ends with the britches and tail area.

Brushing

Brushing your Siberian Husky daily during shedding season removes dead hair and offers some relief from the clouds of Siberian undercoat invading your home. Use a rubber-based wire slicker brush and a shedding rake to remove dead undercoat from your dog. A Greyhound-style comb helps to produce a finished appearance. Pay particular attention to your dog's chest and neck areas, which require the most diligence to remove all the dead hair.

How to Brush Your Siberian

Most dogs dislike having their legs and feet brushed but particularly enjoy having their backs and rumps brushed. Therefore, begin and end your brushing session by brushing your Siberian's back and rump.

Use a grooming table with a nonskid surface.

When your Siberian is not "blowing his coat" during shedding season, a quick going-over with a slicker brush a few times a week will keep his coat in healthy condition.

Use a fine-toothed flea comb to check for the presence of fleas and ticks in your dog's coat, and to remove any flea dirt present in the coat. Check his coat for dryness or bald spots, and inspect his skin for injuries, scaliness, or hot spots.

Breeders do not recommend any trimming, shaving, or clipping of the Siberian coat.

Bathing

Due to the natural cleanliness of the Siberian Husky coat, as well as the fastidious nature of the breed, treat bathing your dog as an option to be considered a couple of times a year, if necessary.

How to Bathe Your Siberian

Always select a shampoo made for dogs, and rinse it completely

Rinse your Siberian well after shampooing him.

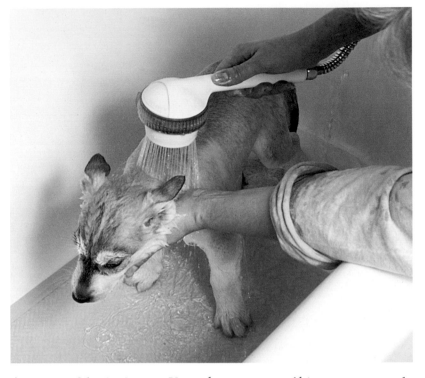

Flea Free

Fleas present a challenge to keeping your dog healthy and well groomed, as well as a challenge to maintaining your dog's environment. Fleas spend about 80 percent of their time in their surroundings, not on the host dog. Therefore, treating your dog's habitat is a critical element of controlling fleas. Traditional flea treatments, including the newer spot-on liquids, contain pesticides that work by entering a dog's skin; they should not be used on any animal with existing health problems. If you prefer a more natural approach, consult your holistic veterinarian for information about herbal products for flea control.

from your Siberian's coat. Keep shampoo out of his eyes, ears, and nose. Towel dry your dog's coat, and blow-dry it completely. Wild canids have more oil in their fur than domestic dogs, allowing their coats to expel moisture more rapidly and dry faster. Many domestic dogs become stressed when they are wet for a long period, so be sure to dry your dog thoroughly.

A warm bath during shedding season, combined with a brush-out and the use of a shedding rake, may lessen the intensity of the shedding process.

NAIL TRIMMING

When a dog's toenails grow too long, they cause his toes to turn sideways, altering the way that he moves and throwing his skeletal alignment out of balance. The result can result in a painful misalignment of the dog's body structure, leading to compensations in movement that can, in turn, develop into even more severe skeletal problems. Long toenails can also become caught in carpet loops and fringe, blankets on the bed, or in the threshold of a car's doorway, resulting in injury.

Before you begin, consider the length of toenail that's best for your Siberian's lifestyle. A working dog may require a bit more toenail length to provide traction in the snow and ice. The owner of a show dog may shorten her dog's nails to enhance the arch and appearance of the foot. The pet dog owner may keep her dog's nails shorter and rounded to reduce the risk of the dog scratching a member of the family. Always shorten your Siberian's nails in small increments.

How to Trim Your Siberian's Nails

Choose a guillotine- or scissor-style nail clipper. Many dogs tolerate an electric rotary filing tool that grinds down the nails better than nail clippers.

Using your nail cutting tool of choice, snip or grind the nail to a point where you have not cut into the quick. (If your Siberian's toenails are black, you will not be able to see the "quick," or the embedded capillary that delivers blood to the nail. In light-colored, translucent toenails, the quick is visible as a light pink thread originating at the base of the nail and growing out almost to the end of the nail.) If you do trim the end of the quick, and your Siberian's nail bleeds, don't panic! Apply a clotting powder to stop the bleeding, or press a paper towel wet with cool water against the cut edge of the nail for a few minutes. The bleeding should stop shortly.

Well-trimmed nails promote foot health.

The Hair of the Dog

It's shedding season, and your Siberian Husky is releasing clouds of undercoat. Why not put it all to good use and have your Siberian's hair spun into yarn and made into a garment? Warmer than sheep's wool, yarn spun from dog hair is called *chiengora*. A Siberian's fine, lustrous undercoat lends itself perfectly to spinning, although it does not have the elasticity for some projects, like socks. Spun correctly, a dog-hair garment sheds very little and doesn't pill; instead, it fluffs into a beautiful halo of fur. Mass production machinery cannot handle spinning dog hair, so preparation of the hair and spinning it into yarn is performed by hand. The high-quality diets, clean surroundings, regular grooming, and good health care experienced by contemporary Siberians all produce an exquisite coat of hair that has exceptional shine.

Visit Internet sites for information about how to have your Siberian's hair spun into yarn.

Don't push your dog beyond his tolerance limit for this part of the grooming regimen. If he dislikes having his nails trimmed, clip toenails in a session when you will conduct no other grooming activity. Talk to your dog as you work, stay calm, and generously reward all his efforts to tolerate the procedure. Stop the process if your dog becomes agitated, and take a break, even if it means only clipping a couple of nails at a time. After clipping, smooth any sharp edges of the nail with a nail file or large emery board.

If you cannot maintain your dog's nails at a healthy length, enlist the aid of a breeder, your veterinarian, or a professional groomer, but don't neglect this important aspect of caring for your Siberian Husky.

During your nail trimming procedure, make a quick examination of your Siberian's paws. Check on and between the pads for cuts; foreign objects lodged between the toes, such as briars or splinters; and for any sign of an infection or ulceration.

EYE CARE

For the Siberian Husky, eye health is critical to the dog's ability to function outdoors as an athlete. Bring any concerns that you may have regarding your Siberian's eyes or vision to the attention of your veterinarian quickly. For example, if your Siberian paws at his eye or if you notice an overabundance of matter or a red color around his eyes, take action.

How to Care for Your Siberian's Eyes

During a grooming session, check your Siberian's eyes for the presence of hairs, foreign objects, and discharge that can accumulate in their inside corners.

To remove any brown stains from underneath your dog's eyes, gently wipe them with a cotton ball moistened with warm water. For stubborn stains, purchase an eye stain remover made especially for dogs, and use a few drops on your cotton ball.

If your dog's eyes are red, swollen, or contain discharge, consult your veterinarian. It's best not to tamper with your dog's eyes.

EAR CARE

The Siberian Husky's upright ears permit sunlight to enter the outer ear and allow plenty of air to circulate in the ear, helping it to stay naturally clean and free of infection and parasites. A dog's ear canal is considerably longer than a human's ear canal, and it makes a right turn before reaching the eardrum. Therefore, complete examination of a dog's ear canal all the way to the eardrum requires a veterinarian to use an otoscope equipped with special cones.

The Siberian's upright ears allow plenty of air to circulate, helping them to stay naturally clean.

Dogs contract bacteria, fungus, and yeast infections in their ears when these opportunistic organisms proliferate in the warm, moist, dark, and alkaline environment of the ear. Small amounts of these organisms may be present in a healthy ear, but certain conditions may cause them to become pathogenic, resulting in an ear infection in your dog. Ear infections can rapidly become painful and out of control, so check your Siberian regularly for the presence of excessive wax buildup, tarry discharge, ulcers in the ear, strong odor, redness, and other signs of ear problems.

How to Care for Your Siberian's Ears

Some Siberians may have ear hair that grows down into their ear canal. This ear hair tends to catch and hold debris and earwax, which creates conditions favorable for the development of an infection. Pull out hair growing in the ear canal with your fingers or with tweezers. Be patient, because this procedure causes some discomfort for the dog. Never pull out ear hair from a dog who exhibits any signs of an ear infection, whose ears are sensitive to the touch, or who scratches at his ears. Instead, consult your veterinarian for treatment.

To perform normal maintenance cleaning of your Siberian's ears, moisten a cotton ball with an acidic ear cleanser that does not contain alcohol. Select a commercial product made especially for cleaning a dog's ears, use green tea brewed as you would for drinking and cooled to room temperature, or use a few drops of white vinegar dissolved in about ¼ cup (59.1 m) of water. Don't pour the cleanser directly into the dog's ear, which washes any debris down into the ear canal and deposits it on the eardrum. The buildup of wax and dirt will then irritate the lower ear canal and eardrum. Rather, hold the moistened cotton ball between your thumb and index finger, gently push it down into the top of the ear canal opening, and scoop upward. Do not push cotton balls or any other object past the entry of your dog's ear canal. Use a dry cotton ball to clean out any waxy buildup. If you find excessive discharge in your dog's ears even after performing a routine cleaning, your veterinarian may need to flush them using an ear syringe.

Ear mites are tiny parasites. They suck blood from the interior of a dog's ears and fill them with waste matter that looks like black coffee grounds. Their bites ulcerate the ear canal, cause intense itching, and possibly lead to secondary infections. If your Siberian's ears appear to itch intensely, especially when you are cleaning them, your dog may have ear mites. To confirm your

Signs of Oral or Dental Disease in Dogs

Signs of Oral or Dental Disease in Dogs
- bad breath
- bleeding from the mouth
- drooling or dropping food from the mouth
- loose teeth, stained or discolored teeth, or teeth covered in tartar
- loss of appetite or loss of weight
- shying away from having mouth touched or examined

suspicion, place some ear debris from your dog on a white paper towel and wet it with hydrogen peroxide. If you see a brownish red stain on the paper towel when you smear it, the ear debris contains digested blood from ear mites and your dog's ears are harboring an ear mite infection.

Defeat ear mites by using an eyedropper to place a few drops of mineral oil in each ear a few times a week. The oil smothers and starves the mites. Do not use olive oil, vegetable oil, or herbal oils, which may actually feed the mites and are not heavy enough to smother them. If the ear mite infection does not clear shortly or has already become advanced, your veterinarian can prescribe a pesticide to eliminate the problem.

Chronic ear problems may indicate a food allergy or hypothyroidism in your Siberian. Choose the highest quality foods that do not contain chemical preservatives, flavorings, or colorings, or prepare a simple homemade diet for your dog. Ask your veterinarian to check your dog's thyroid if ear infections constantly plague your Siberian. Remember that chronic ear infections may indicate a more generalized health issue that deserves immediate attention.

DENTAL CARE

Siberian Huskies, like most larger dogs, have adequate space in their mouths for their big teeth. However, their powerful jaws might be the cause of more tooth cracks and fractures than smaller dogs experience. And a buildup of plaque and calculus threatens the oral health of all dogs, large and small.

Caring for your Siberian's teeth and mouth consists of cleaning his teeth daily, checking regularly for broken or cracked teeth,

The VOHC authorizes the display of the VOHC registered seal on products intended to help to retard plaque and tartar on the teeth of animals when used as directed. Although this seal does not guarantee the safety of the product, it does indicate that the product met the VOHC standards for effectiveness in retarding the formation of buildup on animal teeth.

and being mindful of tenderness, pain, or any unwillingness that your dog displays to use his mouth for eating or play that may indicate an oral health problem. Also, providing your dog with dental chews may help keep his teeth in good condition. Nylabone makes some good chews that are suited to a Husky's size and chewing power.

The American Veterinary Dental Society (AVDS) reports that more than 80 percent of dogs develop gum disease by the age of three years. In addition, the two most common health problems seen in dogs over seven years of age are periodontitis (inflammation of the tissues surrounding a dog's teeth) and the accumulation of dental calculus (mineral salts found in a dog's saliva). When calculus builds up on the surface of a dog's teeth, it offers surface irregularities on which bacteria adhere, resulting in the formation of plaque. Plaque provides an environment that promotes bacterial growth, causing irritation and infection in the dog's mouth. Veterinarians believe that dental disease in dogs predisposes them to heart disease, diabetes, respiratory ailments, and diseases of chronic inflammation, like arthritis, because this condition releases harmful bacteria into the dog's bloodstream.

How to Care for Your Siberian's Teeth

Daily cleaning of your Siberian's teeth is the key to reducing the incidence of dental disease in your dog. However, even with diligent, daily care, your Siberian may require professional dental cleanings during his lifetime, just like humans do. However, cleaning his teeth at home every day will drastically reduce the number of professional dental cleanings required, as well as make a significant contribution to his overall good health.

Introduce your Siberian to tooth care gradually, gently, and as early in life as possible. Begin by just rubbing your finger over your puppy's teeth and gums. Approach him from the side, not the front, to make the experience less confrontational. At this stage, you do not need to force your dog's mouth open. You can just lift his lips and cheek and run your finger along his teeth and gums.

Some owners use a soft-bristled toothbrush made for dogs or a soft toothbrush made for a child to brush their dog's teeth. Some owners find that their pets allow them to use an electric toothbrush to brush their teeth, if the owner starts this practice at an early age. Pet supply retailers offer convenient pet toothbrushes that fit over your finger. Some veterinary dentists suggest that brushes polish better than they clean, and recommend the use of a piece of cotton gauze or a folder over piece of cloth that resembles cotton gauze in texture. When using a fingerbrush, gauze, or a cloth, don't rub hard enough to damage your dog's gums. You may decide to experiment to find a tool and a method that works best for you and your Siberian.

Toothpaste made for dogs is readily available in pet supply shops. Oral cleansing gels that contain zinc and vitamin C (which breaks the physical bond between the calculus and your dog's teeth) are also on the market. These products expedite the removal of minor amounts of calculus and plaque already present on your dog's teeth.

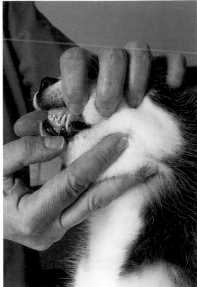

Caring for your Siberian's teeth includes inspecting and cleaning them daily.

If you use toothpaste, select a product made especially for dogs. Human toothpaste contains foaming agents and detergents that are meant to be spit out or rinsed away, and they can be irritating to your dog's stomach. You will not be able to rinse your dog's mouth after brushing his teeth, and he will not be able to spit out the excess toothpaste.

Concentrate your cleaning on the point where the tooth meets the gum. Also, pay special attention to the outside of the upper teeth, which trap most tartar (hardened plaque). If your dog resists this treatment, start with a few teeth and gradually work your way around his mouth in several sessions. Then gradually work up to cleaning all his teeth in one session. Praise your Siberian for his acceptance of your care of his teeth, and have lots of treats handy to reward good grooming-table behavior.

Even if you clean your dog's teeth daily, schedule a veterinary examination that includes a thorough evaluation of his oral health every year. Your veterinarian will check for gum disease and cracked and loose teeth, and will advise you about the effectiveness of your Siberian's home dental care program.

As you develop your regular grooming regimen with your Siberian, enjoy the time that it affords you to share a few moments together. When you groom your dog, you contribute to his overall training in good manners, help to establish your leadership role in his life, and have the opportunity to admire the spectacular natural beauty of your Siberian Husky.

TRAINING *and* BEHAVIOR
of Your Siberian Husky

The knowledge and science of contemporary dog behavior and training have shed new light on the process of incorporating a companion or working dog into a human family. The myth of a Lassie-type dog who is "morally" good, devotedly obedient, and capable of independently evaluating a wide variety of situations and making proper choices (in the eyes of his human owners) has dissolved into the fiction it really always was. Modern animal behaviorists now know much more about how real canines behave and learn.

As the owner of a Siberian Husky, your success rests on your ability to learn about the basic needs of your dog in particular and about how dogs learn in general. You want to accomplish these things, of course, with the least amount of wear and tear on your Siberian so that he fits into human society and your family without totally subjugating his exquisite nature or overpowering his lovely temperament and spirit.

THE FOUNDATIONAL ELEMENTS OF RAISING A GREAT SIBERIAN HUSKY

Before you delve into the details of managing and training your Siberian, consider the ingredients that will form the foundation of success for all your specific training programs. These ingredients will build a strong relationship or bond with your Siberian. Whether you are working on housetraining, advanced obedience exercises, or racing your sled team, these ingredients combine to create a basic recipe for success with your Siberian Husky.

Build Trust

Extremely forceful or intimidating tactics create fear and confusion, not cooperation and obedience. Always use training methods that respect the nature of your Siberian Husky and that are based on a knowledge and understanding of canine learning.

Never lie to your dog. If, just once, you call your dog to come to you and then punish

Always use training methods that respect the nature of your Siberian Husky.

him for something that he did a few minutes ago, years will pass before you may be able to achieve a reliable "come when called." A dog without lies in his life comes when he's called, never flinches when you reach for him, does not hesitate with his responses, and bravely handles difficult or scary situations because he trusts that you always have his best interest in mind.

Devote Frequent Time and Attention

We develop strong bonds with people in whose company we often find ourselves. We fondly relate to family members and coworkers because we regularly engage in mutually satisfying activities in the company of these people. Whether you spend time training, playing with, sledding with, traveling with, or just having your Siberian lie at your feet while you watch television, each moment spent with your dog firmly cements a new building block into the foundation of your good relationship.

Communicate With Clarity and Consistency

Lacking the tool of oral language with which to communicate with dogs, owners can learn the body language, behavioral cues, subtle physical signals, and other means of communication utilized among canines. Not only does a highly successful dog trainer learn to read these canine communications when her dog exhibits them, she learns to use these communication techniques herself to

The Dog Owner's Training Toolbox

With the help of a few basic but highly useful tools, you can manage your dog's behavior, teach new behaviors, and have great fun with him:

- **Crate:** Your Siberian's private place when at home, as well as his home away from home when on the road.

- **Portable doggy playpen or exercise pen:** A place where you can park your puppy when you can't watch him diligently. When placed in the kitchen or a corner of the living room, he can stay close to the activities of the household, have a bit more room to stretch out, and stay out of trouble at the same time.

- **Short, long, and retractable leashes:** Besides its usefulness for outdoor walks, a 6-foot (1.8-m) leash serves as an indoor tether or umbilical cord for your new puppy. A tether keeps your dog under your direct supervision for a short time while you are occupied with other business. A 10- to 20-foot (3.0- to 6.1-m) leash allows you to safely teach behaviors to your dog when he is more than 6 feet (1.8 m) from you. Retractable leashes provide a handy tool for walking your dog where he has plenty of room to explore (not on a busy sidewalk).

- **Car restraint:** Use a crate for your dog when traveling by car. If your vehicle cannot accommodate a dog crate, purchase a car safety belt made for dogs.

- **Collar and identification:** Place an identification tag on your dog's collar. It may be his ticket home someday. Consider having him microchipped as a permanent method of identification.

- **No-pull walking harness:** The Siberian Husky is a pulling breed, and you don't want your walks spoiled by being dragged down the sidewalk. No-pull walking harnesses humanely control pulling on the leash.

- **Clicker:** A small, inexpensive device that makes a clicking noise; it's used as a reward marker for dog training.

- **Treats and toys:** Use high-value treats, such as string cheese, hot dog pieces, or commercially available natural goodies made for dogs, like freeze-dried liver or beef jerky. Provide chew toys, tug toys, retrieving toys, and interactive toys if they appeal to your dog. Remember, though, interactive toys are no substitute for time spent with you!

deepen the quality of her relationship with her dog. A dog who feels confident that his owner can read and understand his point of view about aspects of his environment tends to interact and learn with more confidence and ease. A dog who feels confident that he consistently will be able to make sense of the signals directed at him by his owner will value and pay close attention to those signals.

Train Based on Valuable Rewards

Although dogs enjoy praise and human interaction, asking your Siberian to deliver requested behaviors, modify existing behaviors, or learn complex new skills goes beyond bonding and requires high-value rewards. Manipulating the consequences of the dog's actions so that valued, positive rewards follow desired behaviors underpins good dog training. Identify the consequences that your dog finds the most rewarding, like a game of tug, a piece of cheese, or a romp with other dogs in the household. Modern dog training is based on positive reinforcement techniques—reward good behaviors, ignore bad.

Accommodate Your Siberian's "Hardwiring"

If you own a Siberian Husky, you own a dog who, first and foremost, yearns to pull and lives to run. Period. These characteristics result from years of selective breeding that firmly established them. If you plan to hike with your dog and expect him not to run freely when he's off-lead, save yourself a world of frustration and get another breed. However, if you enjoy cross-country skiing and look forward to the thrill of having your Siberian pull you over endless drifts of sparkling white snow, all his canine hardwiring supports your goal. Your particular Siberian may tire easily of the company of children, go wild for liver treats, have a strong urge to dig, and dislike wet feet. These characteristics result from your particular Siberian's unique personality. Either way, expecting your dog to abandon traits hardwired into his being or resulting from his unique and individual nature invites frustration and aggravation into your life. Developing a training program that works with and through the unique characteristics of the Siberian Husky sets the stage for success.

REWARD-BASED TRAINING: CLICK OR SAY "YES!"

Reward-based training relies on the principle that dogs perform behaviors that produce timely rewards *desired by the dog*. The principle also suggests that behaviors that do not reward the dog naturally extinguish themselves. The theory appears simple enough but contains some complexities, the chief one being that the dog, not the handler, must perceive the reward as desirable. So if your dog constantly jumps up on you and you push him off, but your

dog doesn't get very much other interaction with you at any time, then having you push him off a few times becomes a sort of reward for your dog; he gets your attention and physical interaction for a minute, even if it's in the form of pushing him off.

Contemporary dog trainers use a simple device called a "clicker" to act as a "reward marker" for the dog. Clickers are available from pet shops and dog supply catalogs. The dog learns that the clicker sound means a reward is coming. The sound precisely marks the moment the dog offers a desired behavior in a training session and tells the dog that a reward is now on the way. The clicker makes your indications of correct or desired behavior very easy for the dog to understand. Because we talk to our dogs all day, calling them "good buddy" and "such a good girl," phrases like "good dog" become diluted and no longer operate as highly effective training aids. Something more precise is required: a clicker.

If you do not have access to a clicker when training your Siberian, select a single word that you will use to precisely indicate a correct behavior in a training session. Don't use the word for any other reason. Trainers commonly use the word "yes" for this

Siberian Huskies are hardwired to love pulling and running.

The ability to communicate well with others ranks high as an important skill among canines.

purpose.

Teaching your dog the meaning of the clicker/yes is the first step in your training program. Trainers refer to this step as "charging up the clicker" or "conditioning the dog to the reward marker." Simply click the clicker/say yes one time, and give your dog a treat. Repeat several times and in several sessions. You are teaching your dog that a click/yes means that a treat is coming right away. Easy enough. Your dog doesn't have to do anything at all at this point.

Most dogs catch on readily. When you click/yes, and your Siberian's eyes instantly light up, his head swerves around, and he looks for the coming treat, you have successfully activated one of your most useful training tools.

The chain of events for training behaviors is:

1. Get the dog to do the desired behavior.
2. Click/yes to indicate that he has performed the desired behavior.
3. Reward and release by saying "Okay," the signal that the exercise is finished for now.
4. Add the signal or command word to the desired behavior.
5. After the dog makes the connection between the signal word and the behavior, use the signal word to get him to perform the desired behavior.
6. Generalize the behavior by asking the dog to perform it in many different places.

TYPES OF BASIC DOG CONTROL

Generally, the areas in which you will establish basic control and train desired foundational skills and behaviors in your Siberian Husky fall into these categories:

- **Communication:** Learning and using signals and cues to anticipate and understand your Siberian's state of mind and the reasons for his behaviors.
- **Socialization:** Preparing your Siberian Husky to fit smoothly into human society.
- **Play:** Teaching your Siberian the rules of appropriate play behaviors.
- **Basic Household Manners:** Managing the daily living circumstances of your Siberian Husky and teaching him how to behave as a successful member of your household.
- **Obedience Training:** Teaching your Siberian to respond to specific signals to deliver specific, desired behaviors.

Make a commitment to read books and articles about these subject areas, attend good-quality dog training classes, or join breed or dog training clubs. They will help you to become adept in these important aspects of contemporary dog training.

COMMUNICATION

To communicate with others of their species, dogs use a unique and universal vocabulary of body language, made up of subtle signals, cues, and various indications of their state of mind. The ability to communicate with others quickly and without any misunderstandings ranks high as an important skill among social species and pack animals like canines. Skilled canines readily avoid conflict with other canines, easily defuse stressful situations, and successfully inform other members of their species about their intentions in advance. These easily recognized communications skills lubricate the many daily interactions in the group and allow each canine to broadcast his intentions quickly, even to strangers.

Although your Siberian will learn to respond to your verbal communications, he also will manifest these canine indicators in his interactions with you. If you learn to read them reliably and use them yourself, your dog will develop confidence about the quality and predictability of your interactions with him. If you ignore this subtle canine body language, your Siberian will abandon it in your presence, in sheer frustration.

Canines signal friendliness, lack of aggression, and a desire for calm by turning their heads to the side, averting a direct stare by sliding their eyes to the side, turning their flank or back to another dog, quickly licking their noses, walking or moving slowly or

Learning About Clicker Training

Many websites and dog training books are devoted to the science of clicker training, a system for teaching behaviors using positive reinforcement techniques. Made popular by Karen Pryor, formerly a dolphin trainer, her website www.clickertraining.com offers advice and instruction for the beginner and advanced dog trainer.

Clicker training builds wanted behaviors in your dog, rather than focusing on how to stop or eliminate unwanted behaviors. Once you get the hang of it, you and your dog will become partners in his training process.

in a curved path, and freezing in place. They indicate a need to relax by sitting or lying down, yawning, or sniffing the ground excessively. They invite play by bowing their front ends down to the ground. Dogs show submission by crouching down to make themselves appear smaller, by licking the mouth of another dog, blinking their eyes, and lifting their paw. Raised hackles and tails indicate excitement, and showing teeth, barking, and growling give warnings of aggressive intentions.

You can use some of these signals to understand and manage your dog's behavior. When children push your Siberian beyond the limits of his endurance, watch for the subtle signs of his distress and answer him back by approaching him from the side in a curved path. Speak to him softly, and do not crouch over him or talk directly into his face. Remove him from the situation and allow him to calm down. If you want to start a play session, get down on the floor and perform a play bow. Your dog instantly will know what's happening! If your dog appears stressed in a group of other dogs, step between your dog and the others. Put your back to the other dogs to signal them to stay calm, and escort your dog away from the melee using slow movements.

SOCIALIZATION

Socialization is the process of habituating your dog to many environments through repeated, positive exposures to those environments. Most dog owners and trainers would rather have a well-socialized dog than a well-trained dog, and they consider proper socialization the best single investment you can make in your canine companion. You can work through all the obedience training in the world, but if your dog is fearful of new situations and lacks confidence and social interaction skills, his deficiency of proper socialization will always work against his future behavioral and training outcomes.

The key socialization period for the Siberian Husky (and other domestic dogs, depending on the breed and the individual dog) generally runs from birth to about five months.

Socialization Inside the Home

Invite visits from your family and friends soon after bringing your Siberian Husky into your home. Your puppy will start by meeting new people in a safe, familiar place. Tell your visitors that you are socializing your puppy so that they will understand that all of their interactions with your Siberian should be positive and fun. Monitor these interactions, and reward your young Siberian for good behavior, like calmly accepting approaches from your visitors and taking treats from their hands. Allow your visitors to bring their friendly, reliable dogs to your home. Carefully manage their interactions with your puppy, and don't overdo it. Watch your Siberian as he learns to use canine body language and communicate with his canine visitor, and notice how his canine visitor responds.

Socialization Outside the Home

Now it's time to take your socialization activities on the road. Start with visiting "easy" places and meeting "easy" people or animals for short periods. Easy places include a friend's quiet home, banks, libraries, and malls in the morning. Easy people include people who resemble the members of the puppy's family. Easy animals include reliable, well-behaved pets belonging to members of your extended family or good friends. These socialization sessions should start at two to three minutes each. Carefully observe your Siberian's reaction to his experiences and the new environment.

Watch your Siberian's body language for signs of stress (tucking his tail, yawning, withdrawing, losing focus, licking his mouth, shaking). If you are holding your puppy in your arms, keep alert for an accelerated heartbeat. When you see any of these signs of taking on too much too soon, stop the process, but do not go home just yet. Retreat to a quiet place where your Siberian feels comfortable, and allow him to regain his composure. Ask for one

Your dog should be well socialized to other canines.

more "easy interaction," and then go home. This approach teaches your dog that exhibiting fearful or avoidance behaviors will not release him from a situation completely, although you will honor his need to collect himself. He must learn to calmly handle these situations.

Bring along plenty of treats to reinforce his courage and good behaviors, and tell him "That's right" when he acts appropriately. Have strangers feed him some goodies. Be vigilant against negative experiences, like being handled by teenagers who may be too rough with a puppy.

Use no corrections at all during the socialization process. If your puppy nips at a stranger, remove him from the situation and take a time-out. The next time your puppy behaves well toward a stranger, reward him copiously with lots of treats.

After a couple weeks, graduate your Siberian to experiencing difficult places and difficult people for a bit more time. Difficult places include busy parking lots, city streets, pet shops, and outdoor festivals. Difficult people include children, heavily perfumed women, large, gruff men, and the elderly. These socialization sessions can run from five to ten minutes. Repeat the process at a pace that suits your puppy and that ensures a positive experience every time. When you see signs of stress, back up to the last point of success and proceed more slowly. Be generous with your treats and encouragement. Always ask yourself "Is what I am requiring of my puppy fair at this point?"

How to Avoid Socialization Errors

Do not socialize your puppy at off-lead dog parks; in places where you cannot watch him every second; where he will be too hot or too cold; where large groups of rowdy people are likely to act aggressively, like at sporting events; or where he will meet stray or sick dogs. Always be certain that your puppy will be welcome before you take him to a new destination.

Avoid the common pitfall of inadvertently reinforcing or rewarding your Siberian for antisocial behavior during the socialization process. When your young dog growls at a stranger, you may be tempted to calm and reassure your pet by petting him and soothing him in a soft tone of voice. Your puppy will interpret your reaction as approval of his defensive behavior, namely growling at strangers. The proper time to reward your puppy with praise, reassurance, and plenty of treats is at the moment when he is behaving in a proper manner, as when he willingly accepts the advances of a friendly stranger. If your Siberian acts inappropriately, remove him from the situation, allow your dog to regain his composure, and begin again. Reward him generously for proper behavior.

It is impossible to oversocialize your Siberian Husky, and socialization cannot be left to occur as a result of everyday life. However, you will reap untold benefits for the time and attention you invest in this process and develop a sense of true partnership and enjoy many years with your well-socialized, "take anywhere" Siberian Husky.

PLAY

Engaging in play can be fun, work off a lot of canine energy, and teach self-control and good manners. Playtime will light up your Siberian's eyes, make him tuck his tail with glee, and have him bouncing around the yard in joyful anticipation. It may do the same thing for you! Just remember to structure your Siberian's play to direct his energies into appropriate channels, reward good behaviors, reinforce good habits like curiosity, and keep a sense of lightness and humor in his life. You enrich your entire relationship with your Siberian when you include positive, playful interactions.

Be a Class Act

Dog training classes offer a great opportunity for you to learn the intricacies of dog training while helping to socialize your pet in controlled surroundings. Solicit recommendations for respected training programs from your veterinarian, dog-owning friends, breeder, or from the website of the Association of Pet Dog Trainers (APDT) at www. apdt.com. The APDT certifies companion-dog trainers who have attained proficiency in humane dog training methods, and it emphasizes the importance of lifelong learning for dog training instructors.

A quality dog-training class is both fun and informative!

Each dog has personal play habits and preferences. Some dogs enjoy learning new games all the time, and others find one or two games that really excite them. The line between hard play and aggression blurs on occasion, so always err on the side of caution and disallow any aggressive play responses from your Siberian. Don't grab your Siberian's cheeks, slap at his face, or encourage him to growl or bite at you, your clothing, your children, or his toys during playtime. This often mislabeled "playful aggression" can get your dog into trouble later when a stranger reaches to pet him or when a relative tries to pick up his ball to start a game of fetch.

Keep the energy level in your play sessions low enough so that you do not elicit your dog's aggressive responses. If he crosses the line between play and aggression by grabbing at your clothing, putting his mouth over your hand, body slamming you or another dog, or racing around in a frenzy, immediately but cheerfully stop the game and say "Oops!" or "That's enough for now." Use calming signals, like turning away from your dog and moving slowly and carefully or even freezing in place to signal your desire for your dog to calm down. End the play session without rancor, and wait until your dog regains his composure to begin another one.

Keep your play sessions lighthearted and fun. Remember that these sessions incorporate play activities that indirectly result in the training of desired behaviors, like coming when called and releasing objects to your hand. The sessions are not as well defined as formal obedience training sessions. If you own an older Siberian who has not experienced the fun of well-managed playtime, look for small behaviors that lend themselves to play and encourage them. When your inner child meets your Siberian's inner puppy, the result is a rousing good time!

BASIC HOUSEHOLD MANNERS

Your Siberian Husky can live a very comfortable and happy life as a full-fledged member of your family without turning into a pushy, obnoxious, demanding, and aggravating pet. To accomplish this goal, offer your Siberian a few privileges that he must learn originate from you (not from his own demands) based on his good behavior. When he has earned these privileges, add a few more, and so on, always with the understanding that you control the privileges as a reward for good behavior. Eventually, your dog will earn many freedoms and rewards, but most importantly, he will

Teach your Siberian the rules of appropriate play behaviors.

have learned that you control those privileges, and you will have a pleasant, cooperative canine companion.

Always use positive training techniques, such as praise, food rewards, and lots of attention, to help your Siberian learn what you want him to do. If you reward good behaviors with positive things, his desired behaviors will remain firmly in place.

Crate Training

A crate is an essential tool for managing your Siberian's behavior. Not only will he delight in having his "own room," with a snuggly blanket and a sense of security, but he will enjoy the structured existence offered by the crate.

Why Use a Crate?

When you use a crate properly, you can leave your dog home alone for short periods and not wonder if he will soil or damage the house. A crate also protects your Siberian while you are away and hinders him from developing bad habits when you are not present to manage his behavior. When you are at home, use a crate to confine your dog at times when he may become overexcited or

Purchase a crate that has good ventilation.

get underfoot. For example, when workers arrive at your home or when lots of children show up for a birthday party, a crate does the trick. And of course, a crate establishes the regular routine required to housetrain your dog.

A dog travels safely in a crate; when crated, he cannot distract the driver and will not bolt from the car into traffic as soon as one of the doors open. If you have a fender bender, a crated dog will not run out of the car if a police officer or other safety official opens your car door. If his crate comes along, when you arrive at a motel room or the home of a friend or family member, your Siberian will easily adapt to his new surroundings.

Types of Crates

Purchase a wire mesh crate or a fiberglass or plastic crate with good ventilation. The crate should be large enough to permit your Siberian to stretch out flat on his side without being cramped and to sit up without hitting his head on the top. Some "grow-along" crates have moveable panel inserts to decrease the size of the crate temporarily to accommodate a puppy. (A crate that measures too large for a puppy defeats the purpose of confinement for housetraining purposes.)

Crate Location

Place the crate in a quiet corner of your home, and drape a sheet or light blanket over the top and sides of it to create a den-like atmosphere inside. The master bedroom serves as a great location for a crate, especially if your Siberian will sleep in the crate regularly. If your Siberian will not sleep in his crate or you have absolutely no room for it in your bedroom, the kitchen is a good alternate location.

How to Crate Train Your Siberian

Introduce the crate gradually to a puppy or to an adult dog with no history of crate training. Keep the first associations with the crate especially positive and pleasant. Secure the door of the crate in the open position so that it can't bang shut and frighten your Siberian, and have the crate available to your dog all of the time. Encourage him to investigate the crate; toss in a few treats and let him get the treats, turn, and exit the crate. Praise him enthusiastically. Place his bedding in the crate, and allow him to explore the crate and exit at will. Coax your Siberian to sit down and relax while he's in the crate.

After a few days, close the crate door briefly while you sit next to it. Meet any resistance with pleasant firmness. Remove your dog's collar so that he cannot catch it in the crate's wire mesh, and place a safe bone or chew toy in the crate. Close the door and leave the room for a few minutes without fanfare. Gradually extend the time your dog stays in his crate, up to an hour at a time.

When your dog becomes content in his crate, has demonstrated excellent reliability in his nondestructive behavior when left alone, and has successfully completed his housetraining, you may wish to leave the crate door open at night or throughout the entire day and night. If all goes well, you can now consider the crate your dog's permanent room, available for confinement when circumstances dictate. If you are determined to remove your Siberian's crate after completing his crate training, place his bedding in the spot where you located his crate.

If crate training does not go smoothly at first, don't despair and don't relent! The dog who calmly accepts his crate right from the start is in the vast minority. Be consistent, firm, and pleasant, and remain aware that you are showing your Siberian how to fit into your household, earn many future privileges, and not get into trouble along the way. That fact makes a crate one of the best friends your Siberian will ever have.

Crate Training Don'ts

- Do not release your dog from the crate when he is barking, complaining, pawing at the crate door, or throwing a

tantrum. You do not want him to employ these methods to obtain release from his crate or to learn, in general, that a tantrum produces desirable results. Encourage him to quiet down, and then slowly approach the crate and release him with praise for his calm demeanor.

- Do not use the crate as a form of punishment or "solitary confinement." A dog's crate should be his quiet, comfortable, safe haven, unassociated with any negative connotations. It's a place where he learns to settle down and rest.

- Do not feed your Siberian Husky in his crate because you want to maintain it as a neat, clean, and inviting location where he can relax. The odor of past dinners will only serve as an unwanted stimulus.

- Do not let the crate become a playhouse; instead, it should be a "quiet room" for your Siberian, who deserves privacy in a space of his own. Many dog problems begin when a dog cannot find a single place in the entire house where he can relax and enjoy a moment of privacy. If he naps behind the couch, the children roust him out. If he folds into a corner of the kitchen, Mom jostles him to get access to the pantry. If he tucks into a corner of the dining room, the family shoos him off the expensive carpet. The increased level of daily anxiety produced by this situation leads to canine problem behaviors, such as growling at family members, nipping, and protecting inappropriate places and possessions in the home.

- Do not allow your puppy or adult dog to grow overly protective of his crate. Although the crate is his private place, he should allow an adult family member to reach in and remove him from it without difficulty or any sign of aggression. Practice taking your Siberian from the crate by slowly reaching into it and encouraging him to exit. Be sure to have treats handy to impress on him that leaving his crate at your direction leads to good things, like a yummy treat, and not unpleasant things, like a nail clipping session. If you must remove your Siberian from his crate for a nail clipping session or other somewhat unpleasant activity, remove him from the crate, give him lots of treats and praise, and wait as long as possible to begin the session.

Make every attempt to distance extraction from his crate from the unpleasant activity to follow.

Housetraining

Housetraining requires more from your Siberian Husky than merely learning to control his bladder and bowels until he gets outside. Your dog will be required to discriminate about where he should eliminate (the specified area in the backyard or the location that you indicate when away from home) and where he should not eliminate (in the vegetable garden or on the landscaping in front of your aunt's house). He will also learn to generalize rules about elimination from your home to the rest of the world. (He can't urinate indoors in any house, motel room, or indoor dog-training facility, etc.) Your dog will learn to indicate to you his need to eliminate and then contain his need to eliminate until he reaches an appropriate place designated by you. He also will learn when to eliminate on command in an expedient manner.

As complicated as this list of behaviors sounds, a simple plan for housetraining, implemented with consistency and for a relatively short time, will make easy work of this foundation training.

How to Housetrain Your Siberian

Used in conjunction with a well-thought-out

Crating as Behavior Management Tool

Crating a dog is a behavior management tool, not a method of frequently confining a dog for long hours, for the convenience of his absent owner. For longer confinements, use a properly prepared yard, or the services of a doggy day care center or a home pet-walker.

Some dogs simply cannot tolerate the close confinement of a crate. Often, these are adult dogs who never received proper crate training, senior dogs who have lost their ability to readily adapt to new circumstances, or dogs who have suffered a traumatic experience while confined in a crate. Sometimes a dog will accept a crate as long as the crate door remains open but will object violently when you close the crate door.

The barking and behavior of a panicked dog differs dramatically from the demands of a dog who just wants to get out of his crate and play. A panicked dog barks or howls, non-stop, for hours on end, frantically attempts to bite or claw his way out of the crate, and may urinate or defecate in his crate due to excess stress. Such a dog may injure himself by breaking teeth on the crate bars or ripping out toenails when pawing at the crate's wire mesh.

Take your Siberian outside at regular times so that he learns to eliminate on a schedule.

housetraining program, crating provides the basic method of controlling your Siberian's elimination when you are unable to supervise him. Your dog does not want to live in the presence of his own excrement any more than any other creature does. In fact, he is highly unlikely to soil his sleeping quarters, so place him in his crate when you leave home.

It's helpful to have a puppy playpen or exercise pen (ex-pen) set up in the kitchen or other high-traffic area of the house during housetraining. When you cannot actively supervise your Siberian and prevent him from having an accident in the house, place him in the ex-pen where he can watch the ongoing activity in the house but remain confined. You may wish to "tether" your Siberian to you in an approach often referred to as the "umbilical cord" method. Clip a leash to your dog's collar, and tie the other end around your waist or to your belt. The leash should be long enough to allow your dog to sit or lie down while next to you but short enough so that he cannot make a move to eliminate without your knowledge. The key is to prevent your Siberian from having an accident in the house, whether you can supervise him or not. Every accident that you prevent brings you a step closer to reliable housetraining.

Next, get into a routine and stay there. Establish a seven-day-a-week sleeping, waking, feeding, exercise, play, and elimination schedule. Greet the dawn by taking your dog out right away. Bring him to the designated elimination area first thing in the morning, before and after eating and playing, before you leave home and when you return home, and before bedtime. If you have a very young puppy, take him out every hour or so during the day and stretch the time between elimination breaks as he matures.

Take your dog to the same spot to eliminate. Also, do not turn him out in the yard alone during housetraining. You must be with him to show him exactly where to eliminate. When he eliminates in the correct place, reward him profusely. He'll soon catch on to the idea.

As your puppy begins to understand about eliminating only in a designated area, place a command on the act of elimination. When you have your puppy outside, just before he eliminates, say a command like "Hurry up" that you can use in the future. Your dog will associate the command with the act of eliminating. Later, when you are traveling with your Siberian, you can walk your dog to the designated pet area and give the command "Hurry up." He will understand exactly what you want him to do. Also, having a command for the act of elimination signals to your dog that you are not in this place for play or for an endless sniffing party, but to take care of business.

Learn to read the signs that your Siberian needs to eliminate.

How to Find a Dog Trainer

The Association of Pet Dog Trainers (APDT) is a professional organization of dog trainers that emphasizes education in contemporary training methods for its members. Visit their website (www.apdt.com) for a list of APDT member trainers in your area.

Consult with your veterinarian, dog club members, and other dog enthusiasts in your area for additional referrals. Observe a group class or individual training session conducted by a prospective trainer.

Choose a dog trainer who models the best methods of dog handling and owner counseling. She should do the following:

- Make training your dog fun.
- Demonstrate good teaching skills as well as good dog handling skills.
- Use contemporary, humane methods and tools with the dogs and show courteous respect for the dog owners.
- Ensure the safety of all dogs and handlers by requiring the use of leashes, training in fenced outdoor areas, and removing sick or aggressive dogs from group classes.
- Not guarantee the results of her instruction unless she performs all the training with the dog herself. However, the trainer should guarantee the quality of her professional services.

When he sniffs the floor, acts restless or paces around the house, tries to get your attention, or circles about, take him out immediately. Also, try to anticipate those things that seem to make your puppy need to eliminate, like the kids arriving home from school.

Housetraining Accidents

Never punish your Siberian for an accident, even if you catch him in the act. Just rush him outside and allow him to finish in the appropriate place. Praise and reward him for using the proper elimination area. If your dog piddles on the dining room carpet while you are watching a movie in another room, you have suffered a significant setback in your housetraining program. Until he is housetrained, confine him or don't take your eyes off him.

As your Siberian becomes reliable and has established a track record of avoiding accidents for a few weeks, cautiously increase his freedom in the house. For example, if he proves reliable in his ex-pen in the kitchen, you might use baby gates to enclose the kitchen temporarily and allow him the freedom of the entire kitchen while you are cooking dinner. Go slowly. Address any

Learn to look for signs that your Siberian needs to eliminate, such as sniffing the floor.

lapses by retreating to the last step in your program where your Siberian was reliable, and slowly resume the process.

Stay in touch with reality. Your puppy is an animal whom you are training to maintain control over his need to eliminate at a level as high as most human toddlers can barely manage. Don't expect him to "know better." He's struggling to learn a complex behavior at a very early age.

Patience pays off. With a lot of effort expended for a month or so, you will have built the foundation for reliable housetraining, at home or elsewhere, that will last a lifetime.

BASIC OBEDIENCE TRAINING

The behaviors included in a basic obedience training program— *sit*, *down*, *stay*, *give*, and *let's go*—were not chosen at random. Over the years, experienced handlers defined a few commands that allow you to gain a basic level of control over your dog's behaviors, with the goal of having a dog who functions successfully as a companion pet in human society. These basic behaviors are the cornerstone of good companion dog behavior.

Leash Training

Originally designed to act as a safety device to prevent a dog from chasing another dog or running into traffic, the leash has evolved into a steering instrument used to physically manipulate a dog from one position to another or to physically restrain him from bolting off in all directions. We often see adult dogs dragged along by their owners (or vice versa), pulled away from passing dogs or strangers, and yanked away from interesting but dangerous items lying on the sidewalk, like old gum or cigarette butts. In this respect, the leash unfortunately has become a substitute for training and communication.

With very young puppies who have not yet received their basic obedience training, the leash serves the dual purpose of safety restraint and positioning mechanism. But for the adult dog who has developed a cooperative relationship with his handler through good training and successful, mutual communications, the leash should return to its intended role as a safety measure.

How to Leash Train Your Siberian

After your Siberian Husky puppy has become accustomed to

Dietary Changes

Don't make a lot of changes to your dog's diet while you are housetraining him. Abrupt dietary changes can wreak havoc with a housetraining program.

The leash is designed as a safety device to prevent a dog from getting into trouble and to keep him from potentially dangerous situations.

his collar, clip his 6-foot (1.8-m) leash to it. Allow him to drag the leash around for a short time, then remove it from his collar. Next, clip the leash to your dog's collar and hold the handle end of it. Follow your puppy along wherever he goes. When he springs off in a new direction, he may come to the end of the leash for a moment and balk at the unaccustomed restraint. Assure him that all is well, provide some good treats, and continue to follow him around with the leash in your hand.

Encourage your dog to come with you as you take off in a new direction. Hold the leash handle and signal your dog to come along with you in a direction that he did not intend to take. Remember, be fair and verbally communicate with your dog that you plan to change direction. Encourage him to follow you, and don't jerk him off his feet when he doesn't expect it. If your puppy ignores your signal, walk in the direction that you intended. When the leash tightens, and he turns his attention to you, praise and encourage him to come with you. When he complies, offer a treat reward and walk on.

After a few of these initial training sessions, clip the leash to your puppy's collar and remain still, even if he bounds off. When he comes to the end of the leash, the leash will stop him. Say nothing. He will begin to understand that, when his leash is attached to his collar, he should focus on you, and you will determine the general direction of motion. Now call him to walk a few paces with you, encouraging him all the way. Provide a tasty treat when he comes along.

Watch your Siberian Husky as he walks around the yard off

leash. Most dogs travel from one place to another at a brisk trot. Left to their own devices, dogs rarely walk slowly or amble from one location to another. Maintaining a slow, deliberate walking pace frustrates most dogs, and they quickly lose focus and balk at the lack of speed. Your Siberian will enjoy his introduction to the leash if you indulge his need for speed and keep up a brisk pace as you walk together.

Pulling breeds, like the Siberian Husky, have a strong, instinctive urge to pull against a restraint. Maintain realistic expectations about walking with your Siberian. After all, his natural hardwiring tells him to pull. Using a no-pull walking harness, coupled with the proper training, can solve the problem of humanely and gently managing a Siberian Husky determined to pull while on his leash.

When you signal your dog to sit, you have asked him to settle down and pay attention to you.

Come to Hand: Touch

Teaching your Siberian to come to your open palm and follow your hand allows you to position your dog, without using the leash as a device to physically pull your dog into place.

How to Teach Touch

Place your open hand down at your puppy's eye level, palm toward him. Encourage him to come toward it. When he moves toward your hand, click/yes and reward. Eventually, you want your dog to touch the palm of your hand with his nose, so ask him to come closer and closer to your palm each time before you click/yes. When he comes very close and touches your open palm, click/yes and provide a big reward.

When your dog reliably approaches and touches your open palm, say the verbal signal "Touch" before rewarding your dog. Work on this exercise until he approaches and touches your palm when you place your hand down and say "Touch."

As you work this exercise, you are constructing your invisible leash—an important, nonmaterial connection between you and your dog that operates much more effectively than any 6-foot (1.8-m) ribbon of leather and improves the quality of your communications with your dog as well!

Sit

When you signal your dog to sit, you ask him to settle down and pay attention to you while not requiring him to completely relax "for the long haul." In a *sit*, you bring your dog's focus to you.

How to Teach Sit

Take a treat between your fingers and hold it up to your chest. Most likely, your dog will sit automatically. It will be easier for him to sit and watch for the treat than to stand and crane his neck back to keep an eye on it. Click/yes and reward when your dog sits. Repeat this training a few times. Now your dog knows that when you hold a treat up to your chest and he sits, the clicker goes off and he gets a reward.

Next, when your dog is in the sitting position, say "Sit" one time. Click/yes and reward your dog. Repeat this procedure so that he becomes accustomed to hearing the word "sit" associated with the behavior. Click/yes and reward with a treat each time.

If your dog fails to respond to the *sit* command, place the treat in front of his nose and move it up and over his head. Don't keep repeating the word "sit," because you want your dog to respond to a signal word from you the first time you say it.

Canines do not generalize behaviors very well. If you always work on the *sit* exercise in the den, your puppy may not sit the first time you ask him to sit in the living room. He's not being stubborn or stupid—he's being a dog. Be sure to train in different locations to help your dog understand the overall concept of the *sit* command anytime, anywhere.

Privileged or Spoiled?

Living the canine good life is not the opposite of being in a training program. The training program is the ticket to your canine's life of comfort and privilege. Liberties and indulgences come to the dog who has earned them with good behavior learned through training.

Does your dog direct your behavior more often than you direct his? Does he receive biscuits and treats just for being alive? Has your dog been allowed to indulge in behaviors that you now regret but refuse to reverse? If so, your dog is spoiled, not privileged.

When you signal your dog to stay, you are requiring him to pay attention to you and to remain still.

Stay

When you signal your dog to stay, you ask him to pay attention to you and remain still. Use this signal when you don't want your dog to jump up on people, rush in or out of the doorway, or approach a strange dog.

How to Teach Stay

With your dog at your side, signal him to sit. Without moving, wait a second before you click/yes, reward, and release. If your dog gets up from his sitting position, return him to his *sit*, pause a second again, and reward. Repeat several times. When he reliably stays in place for a second or two, increase the time to a couple of seconds, then to 5, 10, and 30 seconds.

Increase your requirements by placing your dog in a *stay* and moving around to face your dog while standing upright and with your dog's nose directly in front of your knees—what trainers refer to as the "nose to knees" position. Your presence directly in front of your dog helps to keep him in the *stay* position. Return to your dog's side, reward him, and release him from the exercise with the word "okay."

Once your Siberian demonstrates steadiness when you are right in front of him, move one step back during the *stay* exercise. Then move another step back; increase your distance until you are at the end of your 6-foot (1.8-m) leash.

This training demands patience and persistence on your part, because your Siberian would much rather chase you around the yard than learn to sit still. However, if you help him to understand the exercise, work each step so that he experiences success quickly, and reward generously, you will show your dog the value of a little self-discipline in the quality of his life with you.

Down

Down signals that your dog must settle completely and prepare to stay there for a while, if necessary. Combining *down* with a long *stay* teaches your dog to relax and wait while you take care of other business at hand. A more relaxed position than *sit*, the *down* allows you to focus on other things while your dog is quiet.

How to Teach Down

With your Siberian in the *sit* position, use a treat to lure him into a *down*. Hold the treat in front of his nose and slowly move it straight down toward the floor. As your dog lowers his head and starts to move down, click/yes and reward. Each time, wait until your dog gets closer to the floor. When your dog fully attains the *down* position, add the word "down" to the exercise.

Lying down represents a position of subordination for a dog, and many dogs resist the exercise until they learn that the rewards greatly outweigh their concerns about assuming a subordinate position. Some dogs learn this exercise quickly at home while working with their owner but stubbornly refuse a *down* in an obedience class while in the presence of other, strange dogs.

If your Siberian resists the down, lure him under your knee, under a low stool or a coffee table, or under a bench so he must lie down and crawl to get the treat. Proceed at a pace that he accepts, and be persistent. When your dog gets the idea, add the verbal signal "Down" when he gives you the correct behavior. Praise enthusiastically and reward generously.

Come

A dog who comes when called is a pleasure. But you are

competing with a lot of attractive alternatives when you call your dog to you, like a chance to run free, chase a noisy squirrel or the neighbor's cat, visit a female dog in season around the block, and investigate all kinds of smells, sounds, and potential adventures. So be prepared to make it worth his while to choose you instead!

How to Teach Come

Don't tip the balance away from you by calling your dog to you to perform disagreeable tasks, like clipping nails, cleaning ears or teeth, or hustling him into his crate just before you leave the house. For these times, go and get your dog and bring him to you. Otherwise, you jeopardize the strength and reliability of the *come* command.

To teach this command, go to a quiet room in your house where there are few or no distractions. Say "Come" in an inviting tone of voice. Don't shout; simply say "Come" a little louder than normal and with some authority. When your dog comes to you, click/yes and reward him. Practice this exercise several times in each training session, several times a week, and in different rooms of the house.

When your dog is traveling several feet (m) to come to you, start

The down *can be difficult for many dogs to learn, so praise and reward your Siberian generously when he masters this command.*

playing games that support training to come when called. Have someone hold your Siberian in the yard while you take one of his toys and hide it. Let him see you take a toy with you as you leave. Call him using his name, and say "Come." When your dog finds you, excitedly praise him and let him play with the toy.

Have someone hold your Siberian while you start running away with a toy or treat in your hand. When your helper releases your dog, call his name and say "Come." When he reaches you, praise him and toss the toy or treat for him to catch.

Unless you practice in a completely confined area, like a fenced yard, you must have your Siberian on a long line to ensure absolute safety and compliance while training the *come* command.

Always keep in mind that your Siberian retains many generations of "programming" hardwired into his brain. What effect does this programming have on your dog? It tells him to run. It urges him to run. It makes him *need* to run. Therefore, you can offer no reward that will outweigh this need when it urgently surfaces. If you use a leash as a backup safety precaution, you will never have to comb the neighborhood or search the animal shelters for your runaway Siberian Husky.

Let's Go

A trainer uses the *let's go* command to tell her dog to walk with her on a loose leash. The *heel* command denotes a very specific position next to your leg that your dog must maintain consistently while in motion. Heeling has a place in competitive obedience circles, but for a casual walk in the park, *let's go* simply tells your dog to walk along with you without jerking and pulling on the leash.

How to Teach Let's Go

With your Siberian on leash and standing still, toss a treat about 3 feet (0.9 m) behind him. After he turns, goes to the treat, and eats it, click/yes when he returns to you for more goodies. After a few repetitions, repeat the process, only this time, turn and walk away from your dog while he's coming toward you. When your dog catches up to you but has not passed you, say "Let's go" and click/yes and reward. Stop walking after traveling a few paces. Your Siberian will have walked on a loose lead by your side for a few steps.

Gradually increase and randomize the number of steps you take with your dog. When you can walk a reasonable distance without him pulling on the leash, move the training exercise to more distracting places, like out in the yard or on the sidewalk.

If your Siberian Husky continues to pull on leash or pulls when other members of your family walk him on leash, enlist the aid of a no-pull walking harness for the safety and comfort of your family and your dog.

Give

The day will come when your Siberian Husky is carrying something in his mouth that you want him to release immediately. He may have picked up a dead mouse, a piece of horse manure, a cigarette butt, or another dog's toy. Or you may want him to do something as simple as release his own toy during a game of tug.

How to Teach Give

Teaching your dog to give begins as a trading exercise: trading his possession for an especially attractive treat. Have high-value treats ready. Use a toy to play with your dog; when he is holding the toy, say "Give" and hold out the treat to him. When your dog releases the toy, click/yes and give him the treat. *Immediately give him back the toy.* Continue to play with your dog and repeat the training without overdoing it. Practice the training with other items that your dog may carry around, like a stick. He will learn that if he releases something he values to you, he will receive much more in return.

Don't Play This Way!

Stay away from playing with your Siberian in the following ways, to avoid reinforcing undesirable behaviors:

- *Roughhousing:* Don't indulge in games that include hard physical contact, like shoving, or that allow your dog to throw himself at you or jump up on you. Never grab and pull your Siberian by the face, skin, or hair during play.
- *Intense indoor games:* Save throwing balls and madly chasing your dog for the outdoors. Play mind games and more controlled physical games in the house.
- *Chasing laser lights or flashlight beams:* This game elicits obsessive-compulsive behavior that includes chasing any shadow, reflection, flying insect, light source, or beam of sunlight that crosses his vision. These obsessive behaviors can be extremely difficult to eliminate.

Use the leave it *command to keep your Siberian from approaching or picking up something undesirable.*

Leave It

When you anticipate that your Siberian will approach or pick up something undesirable, signal him to stay away from the item with the words "leave it." "Leave it" signals to your dog that he should move on from whatever has piqued his interest at the moment.

How to Teach Leave It

Place your dog on leash or work in a quiet room of the house. You may find it easier to do this training while sitting on the floor or in a chair in front of your dog. Put some low-value treats (like kibble) in one of your hands. Have high-value treats (like cheese) ready in your other hand. Close the hand holding the low-value treats, and put that hand in front of your dog. Your dog will nuzzle your hand to get the low-value treats, but your hand is closed. When he stops trying to get the treats in your hand and turns his head away from your hand, even slightly, say "Leave it" and click/yes. *Reward your dog with the high-value treats in the other hand*, not with the low-value treats.

When your dog reliably turns away from your hand and waits for the high-value treats, practice the exercise with your low-value treat hand open. Say "Leave it." If your dog starts to take the low-value treats, close your hand. Click/yes only when he complies with the *leave it* command, and always reward him with the high value treats.

When your dog has mastered *leave it* working with food in your hands, place a couple of pieces of low-value treats on the floor, and work the exercise again. Continue to reward good performance with high-value treats. Have your dog on leash so that you can prevent him from getting the low-value treats during the training. Remember, you are teaching him that he will receive significant rewards if he forsakes an interesting item that you have asked him to ignore.

PROBLEM BEHAVIORS

Your Siberian Husky brings generations of breed characteristics with him to your home. These breed characteristics may spawn certain unwanted canine behaviors but may prevent others from happening. Relish the fact that you will avoid some behavior problems, and have realistic expectations about the appearance of others. Also, remember that most problem behaviors are "problems" for you but just expressions or exaggerations of normal canine behaviors for your dog.

Bred to be a cooperative member of a sled pulling team, the Siberian Husky relies on his sensible good nature to ensure his success in the group. Problems of dog-to-dog aggression and other dilemmas that arise in multiple-dog households are rare among Siberians. The responsible breeding practices established by the Siberian Husky Club of America have helped to maintain the steady, reasonable temperament of the Siberian Husky, so issues of hyper-shyness, extreme nervousness, unfriendliness to strangers, and inappropriate fear responses also remain uncommon in this breed. Many dogs jump up on their owners and visitors to offer a cheerful and enthusiastic greeting, but Siberians exercise more restraint in this respect than do most other breeds. Also, although your Siberian may release a mournful howl into the evening air on occasion, repetitive nuisance barking is not a common problem.

So what common problem behaviors must the owner of a Siberian Husky prepare to meet? Digging, chewing and destructiveness, pulling on the leash, fence jumping, and running away when off lead top the list. Attempting to eliminate these behaviors from your dog's repertoire will frustrate you to the point of distraction. A better plan consists of providing a safe, acceptable outlet for your dog's instinctive behaviors, coupled with taking measures to anticipate and minimize problems before they become a crisis.

Digging

Define a place where your Siberian can dig in the yard, and let him dig to his heart's content. Use barriers to restrict access to your flower and vegetable gardens and to landscaped areas. If you suspect that your Siberian is digging to find a cool place in the yard to rest, be sure that you have provided enough shade and water in his outdoor area.

Provide plenty of chew toys to satisfy your Siberian's instinctive need to chew.

Chewing and Destructiveness

Lots of exercise and a job to do go a long way toward preventing excessive chewing and destructiveness. Dogs have an instinctive need to chew, so provide plenty of acceptable chew toys, such as Nylabones. Some dogs become ritualistic chewers, meaning that they return to the same forbidden item, like a certain corner of the carpet, to chew again and again. For this type of chewer, either remove the item from his universe for a few weeks, or control your Siberian's access to the object. Roll up the carpet for a while, or place a baby gate across the entrance to the living room to save the piano legs.

Leash Pulling

Use tools like the no-pull walking harness, in conjunction with training, to minimize the amount of pulling on the leash that you must endure. Of course, the most helpful remedy is to provide an outlet for your Siberian's desire to pull. Contact your local breed club and discover the world of sledding and other pulling activities that you can do with your Siberian.

Fence Jumping

Your Siberian will attempt to jump any fencing that encloses his outdoor area. You must create a safe, Siberian-proof containment system for your dog in the form of adequate fencing or an enclosed kennel run.

Running Away

The leash remains one of the most important training tools throughout your dog's entire life, even if you have trained the *come* command extensively. An off-lead Siberian Husky is always a flight risk. Never put your trust in the ability of training to overcome instinct's persistent demands.

Has your dog demonstrated proper housetraining? Does he quickly focus on you when you call for his attention? Does he know the difference between his toys and your possessions? Does he willingly relinquish toys and other objects on your signal? Will he wait until you allow him access to his food bowl, the door to the backyard, and to the car? If so, then he should bask in the fruits of his good behavior: the privileges of the canine good life. Enjoy!

Chapter

7

ADVANCED TRAINING
and ACTIVITIES
With Your Siberian Husky

Once you have established the foundation of socialization and training, you are ready to expand the adventure of owning a Siberian Husky. The Siberian's robust nature, general lack of physical ailments, and amiable temperament make him the perfect companion for several types of advanced training activities, performance sports, and dog therapy work. Not only will your Siberian Husky impress you with his style and ability while participating in these activities, you will deepen your relationship with your dog as you both grow, learn, and work together as a team.

AGILITY

The fastest growing canine sport, dog agility offers handler and dog teams a venue filled with excitement, high-energy competition, complex challenges, and a roaring good time. In 1978, the Crufts International Dog Show added dog agility to its schedule as an entertainment for the spectators between other dog-show events. Its immediate and enthusiastic reception led to the birth of a new dog sport.

Agility tests the athleticism, strategy, speed, and precision of both dogs and owners, as well as their ability to work as a team. The dog agility course looks like a playground for dogs, with colorful tunnels, teeter-totter, jumps, and other equipment, referred to as *obstacles*. The grounds of a dog agility trial look like the site of a medieval jousting tournament, with rainbow-hued tents and sunshades for participants, banners and flags announcing the sponsorship of dog clubs or the wares of vendors, dogs and handlers hustling to their designated rings, and spectators applauding as the dogs perform slick

Agility tests the athleticism, strategy, speed, and precision of both dogs and owners.

maneuvers at top speeds.

In obedience competition, the exercises and the order in which they are performed remain the same from trial to trial. The judge scores the performances of each team, but the handler knows the succession of required obedience exercises in advance of the competition. In agility, the courses are not repeated. Each one is unique, designed by the presiding judge. Until just before running each course, the handler does not know the layout of the obstacles or the sequence for completing the obstacles. Thus, the ability to quickly develop a course strategy represents a significant aspect of the sport.

Several organizations support and sanction dog agility competitions and award titles to dogs who complete the requirements of titling for that organization. Each organization may use slightly different obstacles on the course. For example, some venues use the chute, or closed tunnel, and others do not. Each organization may also have a unique goal in developing its agility program. One organization may value speed over precision, and its open, flowing course layouts may encourage dogs to race between obstacles. Another organization may value precision and teamwork over speed, and its "technical" courses may encourage dogs and handlers to demonstrate how well they execute complex turns and maneuvers. Given the preferences and skills of a handler and dog team, there's an agility format that will suit their style. All agility formats start participants at a beginner, or novice, level and increase the difficulty of the course challenges as the team progresses to more advanced levels.

The sport of dog agility requires short bursts of intense, high-speed execution. Most courses are run in less than 60 seconds. Siberians tend to unfurl their power and energies in long spells and over long distances. Therefore, working with your Siberian and an experienced agility instructor, you will learn to encourage a full expenditure of his energy in a short timeframe, which will help you to succeed in the sport.

If you plan to enter your Siberian Husky in agility competition, confer with your breeder, and select a high-drive puppy. It's easier to mold a high-drive dog into a skilled agility competitor than to create a drive for agility in a relatively sedate dog.

Whether you compete at the top levels of agility competition or simply have fun in your backyard or at a local dog-agility training center, you and your Siberian Husky will build a relationship through agility that will enhance every aspect of your life together.

The Many Worlds of Dog Agility

Several large national venues exist for dog agility competition. Each sanctioning organization delivers its own twist on the sport. One venue might focus on handling skills by favoring "tight" or "technical" courses peppered with dog handling challenges. Another venue might focus on speed by favoring flowing courses where a dog can attain high speeds. Standard course times, or the time it takes the average dog to complete the course, will be lower in these types of courses. A venue might focus on your dog's ability to complete course sequences at a distance from you, the handler, while another may use specific obstacles unique to their venue. Whatever agility challenge you and your dog enjoy, there's an agility venue to provide it for you:

- The American Kennel Club (AKC) at www.akc.org. Accepts AKC-registered purebred dogs only.
- The United States Dog Agility Association (USDAA) at www.usdaa.com. Accepts purebred and mixed-breed dogs.
- The North American Dog Agility Council (NADAC) at www.nadac.com. Accepts purebred and mixed-breed dogs.
- The United Kennel Club (UKC) at www.ukcdogs.com. Accepts purebred and mixed-breed dogs.
- The Australian Shepherd Club of America (ASCA) at www.asca.org. Accepts all purebred breeds and mixed-breed dogs.

The Siberian's robust nature and amiable temperament make him the perfect companion for a variety of sports and activities.

CANINE FREESTYLE

Have you ever asked your dog to dance? Hundreds of dog owners have, and their number is growing fast! The sport of canine freestyle illustrates the training relationship between dog and handler in a new way, as they perform a series of choreographed moves set to music. This discipline beautifully highlights the conformation, fluid movement, and willingness of the dog, as well as the subtle techniques of the handler. The grace of the partners in motion, set to music, awes the crowds every time! Canine freestyle adds the element of art to the world of dog training.

Visit the Canine Freestyle Federation, Inc. (CFF) at www.canine-freestyle.org for information about this popular canine sport. No other competitor will arrive with a canine freestyle companion as elegant as your Siberian Husky!

CANINE GOOD CITIZEN CERTIFICATE

In 1989, the American Kennel Club (AKC) initiated its now immensely popular Canine Good Citizen (CGC) program. Serving as a way to recognize and reward dogs who demonstrate desirable behavior in the community and who serve as role model companion dogs, the Canine Good Citizen certificate has become a sought-after distinction by many owners of purebred dogs.

To participate in the CGC program, puppies and dogs must be old enough to have received their required immunizations. The AKC suggests that puppies be retested once they have reached maturity, because behavior and temperament can evolve over time. You can collect information about CGC training and testing directly from the AKC and manage the training yourself. Many dog clubs and private trainers offer classes specifically designed to prepare a dog for CGC testing.

Once your Siberian has passed the CGC test, send a copy of the test form to the AKC, with a recording fee, and receive a CGC certificate for your dog.

Part One

The CGC program is a two-step process. First, the owner must sign the Responsible Dog Owners Pledge. This document attests that the dog is under the routine care of a veterinarian who will

The Canine Good Citizen program rewards well-trained dogs who demonstrate desirable behaviors.

work with the owner to determine a mutually acceptable health care plan for the dog, and that the owner agrees to take care of her dog's needs for a safe environment, exercise, training, and activities that contribute to a good quality of life. The owner also agrees to model responsible dog ownership by doing things like cleaning up after her pet in public places. The owner must also agree to demonstrate a regard for the rights of others by properly managing her dog.

Part Two

The second part of the CGC program consists of the ten-step CGC test.

Test 1: Accepting a Friendly Stranger

The dog must allow a friendly stranger to approach his handler in an everyday setting. The dog should show no signs of shyness or aggression and should not jump on the stranger or break away from his handler.

Test 2: Sitting Politely for Petting

While in the company of his handler, the dog should allow a friendly stranger to touch him without showing shyness or aggression.

Test 3: Appearance and Grooming

Of course, your Siberian Husky's stunningly handsome appearance will get you off to the right start for this exercise! The evaluator checks the overall condition of the dog, including weight, cleanliness of the coat, and alertness. Using the handler's comb or brush, the evaluator lightly grooms the dog and examines his ears and feet. The handler may encourage and praise the dog throughout the exercise.

Test 4: Out for a Walk on a Loose Lead

While walking with his handler, including turning left and right and reversing direction, the dog must be attentive to the handler and respond to her movements and changes of direction. This exercise tests that the handler is in control of the dog by means other than sheer physical restraint in the form of a constantly tight leash. The handler may talk to the dog and praise

A well-groomed, well-socialized, and well-trained Siberian could make a wonderful therapy dog.

him as they walk together.

Test 5: Walking Through a Crowd

The dog and handler walk around normally and pass close to at least three people (the crowd). The dog should not jump on the crowd members, strain at the leash, or show any sign of shyness or aggression.

Test 6: Sit and Down on Command; Stay in Place

At the beginning of this test, the handler places the dog on a 20-foot (6.1-m) line. The dog must sit and lie down on a signal from his owner. The owner may touch the dog in a way that offers gentle guidance, but she should not force him into position. The evaluator must determine that the dog has responded to the owner's signals to sit or down and has not been physically placed in a *sit* or *down*. When the dog is in either the *sit* or *down* position, the handler tells the dog to stay and walks forward, turns, and returns to the dog. The dog must remain in place until the evaluator indicates that the handler may release the dog.

Test 7: Coming When Called

At a distance of 10 feet (3.0 m) from the dog, the handler calls

the dog to come to her. The dog must respond.

Test 8: Reaction to Another Dog

Well-socialized dogs ace this test of a dog's ability to act politely around other dogs. You and your dog approach another handler and dog team, stop, exchange pleasantries, and continue on your way. Your dog should show no more than a casual interest in the other dog or his handler.

Test 9: Reaction to Distraction

The evaluator presents two common distractions, like knocking over a chair, jogging past the dog, or rolling a dolly or baby stroller in front of him. The dog may show interest and curiosity in the event or be reasonably startled, but he should not panic, run away, or bark. He should show confidence and a relaxed demeanor.

Test 10: Supervised Separation

Your dog must demonstrate that he can be left under the supervision of a friendly, trusted person and still maintain his training responses and general good manners. A tester will hold your dog on his leash for three minutes while you are out of sight. The tester will not pester your dog with excessive talking or petting, but your dog must not continually bark, whine, pace, or attempt to flee.

DOG-ASSISTED THERAPY

Imagine that you became ill and unable to care for yourself at home. Perhaps you required hospitalization for a time or needed long-term care in an institution or assisted-living facility. Imagine how you would feel if you were unable to own, or even to touch, your dog, or any dog, again. Even if you had never owned a dog and were unaware of the many emotional rewards of canine companionship, imagine what a wonderful discovery it would be to find this deeply satisfying feeling at a time when you needed it most in your life.

Dog-assisted therapy attempts to address these issues by bringing the company of dogs to persons living in care facilities, such as hospitals, nursing homes, rehabilitation centers, and other institutions. Dog owners share the comfort and companionship provided by their dogs with the residents of the facility to increase

The Delta Society

Established in 1977, in Portland, Oregon, the Delta Society describes its mission as "improving human health through service and therapy animals." Pioneers in studying and understanding why animals are important to the health and well-being of humans, the Delta Society strives to expand the role of animals in human health care. Its earliest members were primarily veterinary and human health professionals, especially university faculty members. Today, the Delta Society is the source of significant research material and documentation about dog-assisted therapy animal selection, handler training, and treatment plan development. The Delta Society provides standards-based training materials and subject matter experts to work with dog-assisted therapy program managers. Visit the Delta Society website at www.deltasociety.org.

Competitive sports require a great deal of precision and focus.

the emotional well-being of the resident, promote healing, ease loneliness and depression, fight stress, and improve the residents' general quality of life. Owners allow the residents and staff to hug and pet their dogs, talk to their dogs, and even watch their dogs perform tricks.

Many dog clubs offer dog-assisted therapy programs in which club members and their pets visit care facilities on a specified day as a group. Most dog clubs and care facilities prefer dogs who participate in dog-assisted therapy to be evaluated by a nationally recognized organization that tests canines for their suitability for therapy work. These groups check the dog's temperament, his ability to handle stress, his ability to navigate calmly in new and challenging surroundings, and his responsiveness to his owner.

Your well-groomed, well-socialized, and well-trained Siberian Husky may have a future as a wonderful therapy dog. You already know the value of his companionship. Perhaps you can share your treasure with others who could benefit greatly from it as well.

OBEDIENCE

Competitive obedience work requires a more advanced level of precision, focus, and self-control than that required for foundational obedience. In preparation for obedience competition, handler and dog teams train diligently and compete for titles that are permanently recorded by the AKC as a part of their dog's official registered name. The United Kennel Club (UKC) also offers formal obedience competitions, or trials.

In an obedience trial, a licensed judge scores participants and their dogs on their ability to perform specific exercises properly. The AKC has selected these exercises for inclusion in obedience competition because, if a dog can master them, he will have the skills to be a useful and enjoyable companion. Some of the exercises include heeling, or walking on a loose leash in a particular position next to the handler; coming when called; staying in place until directed to move, even in the face of distractions; and retrieving objects and returning them to the handler.

Levels of obedience competition begin with the novice level and progress to the open and utility level. At each level, dog and handler must demonstrate mastery of a certain set of skills by obtaining a qualifying score. Of course, the difficulty of the required skills and precision of the performance increase with each

Dog sports give you and your Siberian an opportunity to bond.

level of competition.

The AKC regards obedience competition as a sport. Observers often attend obedience trials just to view the competition. Therefore, the principles of good sportsmanship should guide the actions of handlers inside and outside the show ring, because they will reflect not only on themselves but will influence the attitude of the general public toward competitive dog training. The AKC, obedience clubs, and obedience-trial competitors disallow any harsh treatment of dogs and discourteous behavior by the participants, all of which result in a bad reputation for the entire sport. Accordingly, obedience competitions are a great place to witness the positive relationship between a dog and his handler that arises from working together as a team.

RALLY

Bridging the gap between the sports of AKC obedience and dog agility, rally has emerged as an enjoyable new game for dog and handler teams. The "course" consists of stations where the dog performs obedience-style behaviors, but handlers can verbally encourage their dogs, use a combination of voice commands and hand signals, and repeat commands. This more relaxed method of handling a dog more closely resembles agility handling than handling for formal obedience competition.

The rally judge sets up a course of designated stations (10 to 20, depending on the level of difficulty of the course). At each station, a printed sign instructs the handler about the skill that his dog must perform at that station, and an arrow indicates the forward direction of the course. At a brisk but normal pace, dog and handler teams move together from station to station, completing the entire sequence of numbered signs at each station. The handler may not touch the dog on the course.

The rally judge designs and sets up each course. She answers any questions from the handler and then evaluates the performance of each exercise as well as the sense of teamwork that exists between dog and handler.

Many dog clubs and training facilities have added instruction for rally competition to their class schedules. Rally represents the latest structured game event that provides dogs and handlers the opportunity to have fun training and competing together. If your Siberian happily performs obedience behaviors and you enjoy

events that offer a relaxed atmosphere and a constantly shifting variety of challenges, rally may be the sport for you!

SKIJORING

Would you like to participate in a winter activity custom-made for athletic handlers and their Siberian Huskies? If so, consider the growing sport of skijoring. A Norwegian word meaning "ski driving," in skijoring, a dog in a harness tows a skier on a line. Compared to dog sledding, or *mushing*, dog owners can enjoy skijoring if they own only one or two dogs and wish to purchase a minimal amount of equipment. With a willing Siberian Husky, a pair of cross-country skis, and the proper harness, lines, and safety gear, you and your Siberian can revel in countless hours of fun in the snow doing what your dog does best—pulling as part of a team.

As with all dog sports, you'll be a step ahead if you research books and websites devoted to skijoring, and if you connect with a mentor or dog club active in the sport. The skijoring and mushing communities are generous with their support of newcomers and experienced handlers alike. You will learn how to build the physical stamina of your Siberian required to prepare him for participating in skijoring. Also, you will learn how to teach your Siberian several simple commands that will help him to pull safely and efficiently.

As the skier and team leader, you must develop the fitness and competencies that will keep you in control while on the trail. A handler who often falls or stops to rest or collect himself quickly becomes a frustration to himself and to his Siberian!

Organized skijoring races usually run between 3 and 10 miles (4.8 and 16.1 km). As such, they can be described as sprint-type events. However, the Alaska Skijoring and Pulk Association offers a few endurance skijoring races in the Alaskan interior that run 20 to 50 miles (32.2 to 80.5 km). (A pulk is a sled pulled by a dog, while a skier, attached to the pulk by a line, skis behind it.) However, you don't have to race to enjoy skijoring.

A standard sled-dog harness properly fitted to your Siberian will double as acceptable equipment for skijoring. New to the market is the European Skijor Harness. The manufacturers claim that the harness is more suitable for skijoring than is a sledding harness because it accommodates the steeper angle of the line between skier and dog, as opposed to the flatter angle of the line between sled

and dog. Retailers also sell booties, dog coats, belly blankets, and other comfort and safety equipment to fit your particular Siberian's needs.

The skier wears a padded skijoring belt. Some belts have leg straps that encircle the upper thighs to hold the belt securely in place. A skijoring line connects you with your dog's harness. It incorporates a bungee, or elastic section, to absorb the shock of starting, stopping, and riding on rough terrain, with a tug line that snaps directly to the dog's skijoring harness. Tug lines can be split to connect more than one dog to the setup.

In warmer climates, some owners have experimented with using a skijoring setup to allow their Siberians to pull them on inline skates or bicycles. As in skijoring in the snow, attention to preparation, proper fit of equipment, safety, and comfort make

Spectator Etiquette at Dog Events

You may wish to visit the site of a dog show or performance event in which you are interested in participating. Remember that the registered exhibitors, although usually very happy to answer questions and direct visitors, have spent a considerable amount of time and money to take part in the event. Participation in this event represents the culmination of their many efforts. Therefore, if you observe a few simple rules of etiquette at the show site, you will learn about the sport while respecting the needs of the competitors:

- Leave your own dog at home.
- Do not pet or touch a dog on the site without the permission of the handler. The handler may have recently groomed the dog for the show ring, or she may want to maintain the dog's focus before entering the performance ring.
- Stay away from the ring entrances and exits to avoid adding to the congestion.
- Do not approach a handler with a question until after she has exited the ring and had a moment to collect her dog, both mentally and physically.
- Wear comfortable shoes and casual clothing.
- Bring your own chair if you plan to spend some time at the event.
- Keep your children, strollers, chairs, and food at least 10 feet (3.0 m) from the perimeter of the ring to avoid distracting dogs as they work.
- Visit the information booths, vendor booths, and grooming areas, and talk with exhibitors during their "down time."

the difference between a fun time and a disappointing experience. Always confirm that you and your dog are welcome on any particular trail or path.

Visit www.mushwithpride.com for bountiful information about dog care, exercise, and training for the sport of skijoring.

SHOWING (CONFORMATION)

The AKC refers to its conformation dog shows as its "signature events." AKC conformation shows focus on the distinctive characteristics of purebred dogs and provide a forum for evaluating purebred-dog breeding stock. By recognizing and rewarding high-quality purebred breeding stock, the AKC helps to preserve the unique qualities of each dog breed. Because neutered purebred dogs cannot participate in a breeding program, these dogs are not eligible to enter AKC conformation shows.

The AKC-recognized parent clubs establish the written breed standards used by AKC judges to appraise each dog within a breed. These standards define everything about the "perfect" specimen of that particular breed, including size, color, temperament, structure, and style of movement. These standards originate from the parent club's description of a dog who possesses the mental and physical qualities necessary to perform the work for which the breed was originally intended and used. Therefore, the Siberian Husky official breed standard, established by the Siberian Husky Club of America (SHCA), describes the optimum dog for pulling medium weight loads over long distances, through the snow and ice, as a member of a dog team.

The Rules

At AKC conformation shows, an AKC-approved judge examines each dog in the entry and ranks him in accordance with the judge's own mental image of the "perfect" dog as defined in the breed standards.

To compete in an AKC conformation show, your Siberian Husky must qualify according to the rules of eligibility:

- The dog must be individually registered with the AKC.
- The dog must be six months of age or older.
- The dog must be an AKC-recognized breed for which the show offers classes.
- The dog must meet all eligibility requirements of the

breed standard.

Male and female dogs compete separately. The show operates on the process of elimination, meaning that a dog who wins in the lower-level classes advances to compete in higher-level classes.

Only the judge can decide whether you show the best dog in any class. However, as the handler, you can present your dog in a way that highlights his positive characteristics and diverts attention away from any faults. First impressions mean a lot at dog shows, and your ability to create a stunning first impression separates you and your dog from the rest of the group and indicates to the judge that your dog is worthy of notice.

How to Help Your Dog Succeed

In addition to handling your dog, you serve as his backdrop. As such, dress to make him stand out. For example, a black dog handled by an owner wearing a black skirt will fade into his owner's attire. Bright, complimentary colors frame a Siberian Husky's white, gray, black, and reddish tones and draw attention to his exquisite lines and flowing movement.

Canine Sports and Safety

Your first priority is, of course, the safety of your Siberian Husky when participating in any canine sporting activity. Although you cannot completely avoid the possibility of injury to your active dog, you can learn to anticipate problems and prepare to manage them in advance by adhering to the following:

- Pay particular attention to your Siberian's feet, especially in wintry conditions. Check and treat footpads for ice buildup, cracks, and sore spots. Provide booties to prevent injury.

- Always provide access to a quiet, dry environment, like a crate, where your dog can rest comfortably at the event site.

- Perfect your handling technique for the sport. Skillful handling that helps your dog to negotiate the challenges of the sport helps to prevent injuries.

- Bring water from home. Drinking water that your dog regularly consumes at home prevents stomach upset at the event site.

- Arrange for regular chiropractic evaluations and treatments if your dog is very active, especially if he is older.

- Consult with your veterinarian about adding supplements to your dog's diet to support his joints and muscles and to provide the energy required to compete.

Also, learn to move in a way that encourages your Siberian to flaunt his lovely gait. If your motions are choppy, with a lot of up and down movement, your dog, silhouetted against your body while in motion, will appear choppy, too.

How to Begin

Begin your conformation showing experience by entering your Siberian Husky in AKC-sanctioned matches, or "pretend" conformation shows made available for exhibitors to practice showing their purebred dogs. Matches operate on a much more informal level than official shows. Many times, match-giving clubs will take entries on-site on the day of the event without the need to pre-register. At a match, you can expose inexperienced dogs to the noise and congestion of a show while learning to get your own nerves under control. AKC-sanctioned matches are run in accordance with the AKC rules and regulations for conformation shows.

Clubs may also offer "fun matches," or matches not specifically sanctioned by the AKC. Although these events usually comply with AKC conformation show practices, the local club has more latitude about how to run a fun match. Some clubs may add other activities to the fun match program, like a Halloween costume competition for matches held in the fall or a pet tricks demonstration.

As always, the SHCA and your local breed club are the best sources of information about showing your Siberian Husky in conformation shows. Many books, clinics, and DVDs also are devoted to instruction about showing dogs in conformation events. You will soon discover that breed showing is as much art as science, and it requires some time to master all its intricacies. But you have arrived at the show with one of the most beautiful breeds of dog in the world. You're already a step ahead!

SLEDDING

Many types of equipment can play the role of a dog sled. You can use a sled on which children slide down snowy hillsides, a

The Siberian Husky loves to run and pull things, making sledding a much-loved sport.

lightweight three-wheeled cart for sledding on terrain without snow, a bicycle, or a traditional dog sled as a vehicle for your Siberian to pull.

Pulling harnesses encircle the dog's neck and go over his back to attach him to a line that connects him with his load. Although traditionally made from leather, contemporary harnesses are made from flat, lightweight nylon webbing that dries quickly and can be washed easily. The properly fitted harness lies close to the dog's body, supporting the optimum transfer of strength from the dog to the load, thus giving him the best mechanical advantage for pulling. Do not select an inexpensive harness without the cross-pieces across the back. The material can twist under constant movement and stress, and the harness can slip out of position. Most harnesses incorporate soft pile material around the neck opening, under the chest, and even under the dog's legs to reduce chafing and provide a sort of bumper against sharp starts and stops.

In the traditional fan hitch, each dog is hitched independently and directly to the sled with his own individual line. In the more popular gang hitch used by today's sled-racing drivers, the dogs are harnessed in pairs on either side of the single gang line that pulls the sled.

Mushers (the people driving the team) place each dog in his position on the team of 7 to 11 dogs based on the natural inclinations and skills of each dog. The lead dog directs the team, followed by the point dogs, who help the lead dog turn the team. Next, the team dogs provide the muscle to move the sled and its load forward. The wheel dogs turn the sled itself and take all the shock distributed along the gang line from stops, starts, and rough riding. The frontmost dogs must be fast, responsive, and highly motivated. The rearmost dogs must be strong, resolute, and even-tempered. A significant portion of the art of running a sled-dog team rests on deciding which dogs to place in which positions.

Formed in 1966, the International Sled Dog Racing Association (ISDRA), a group of sled-dog racing associations, monitors dogsled racing throughout the world. In recent years, heritage sled-dog races, or events that celebrate original racing practices, have proliferated in an effort to keep the sport with original sled-dog breeds alive.

The relationship between a sled dog and his handler is deeply rooted in history and is one that a Siberian Husky owner finds himself in a unique position to experience. Few dog owners can enjoy slipping over the sparkling snow in the soft light of a winter morning or riding through a wildflower-filled meadow, happily pulled along by her beloved companion dog. Born to pull and bred to excel at it, your Siberian needs only the direction of a capable handler to unleash his abilities for your pleasure.

As with skijoring, visit www.mushwithpride.com for bountiful information about dog care, exercise, and training for the sport of sledding.

NONCOMPETITIVE ACTIVITIES

Of course, participating in an organized sport is just one way to enjoy working as a team with your Siberian Husky. Many outdoor activities, such as inline skating, walking, jogging, and biking, when practiced in dog-friendly areas, become more fun when shared with your Siberian. Whether he pulls you while in harness or simply joins you on lead during your morning walk, you will experience the companionship of an enthusiastic partner if you take your Siberian Husky along with you.

Many dog clubs offer unique opportunities to have fun with your pet. Some organize drill teams that perform at local outdoor events, such as festivals and parades. In a dog and handler drill team, dogs and owners execute choreographed maneuvers such as heeling or sitting as a group, or calling dogs one at a time out of a lineup. Some clubs man information booths in shopping malls to share facts about obedience training, neutering, responsible dog ownership, and other topics. They often include demonstrations of basic obedience training skills for visitors to the booth.

Whatever sport or activity you choose, you will find a willing and adept partner in your Siberian Husky. His easy temperament, ability to get along with other dogs, kindness to children, and extraordinary good looks make him a great partner in just about any undertaking you can imagine!

Chapter **8**

HEALTH

of Your Siberian Husky

The Siberian Husky Club of America (SHCA), a group of knowledgeable and devoted guardians of this noble breed, has kept its watchful eye on the Siberian through many generations of selective breeding. As a result of the responsible breeding practices advocated by the club, breeders have maintained the Siberian's genetic basis for naturally robust good health. Lacking the physical exaggerations and overamplifications found in some dog breeds, the Siberian Husky remains a fit and vigorous purebred dog with relatively few genetically linked health problems.

Now, as the guardian of your particular Siberian Husky dog, the responsibility of maintaining his hale and hearty nature throughout all the stages of his life rests in your capable hands.

FINDING A VETERINARIAN

To find a veterinarian, first ask fellow dog owners, local breeders, trainers, and dog club members to recommend someone they trust. Narrow your search to two or three veterinarians respected by the local dog-owning community, and make an appointment to visit each practice.

Look for cleanliness inside and out, and be sure that the staff members are friendly and dressed in clean uniforms. Check that the clinic hours and emergency care accommodations will satisfy your needs.

When you meet with a veterinarian, ask about her qualifications, experience, and interest in holistic veterinary care. Is she open to considering holistic modalities along with conventional treatments? How does she feel about dog owners getting second opinions from another practice? How does she react when dog owners use the

The vet will weigh your Siberian at his first checkup.

Internet to collect information about their dog's condition and possible treatments? Your veterinarian should encourage your efforts to gather information about your Siberian's health from appropriate sources, and she should guide your thinking about any recommendations that you may consider.

Puppy's First Checkup

Have your veterinarian examine your Siberian Husky puppy within 14 days of bringing him home. Bring the medical history of the pup, provided by the breeder, to this examination. The history should contain information about the vaccination schedule and feeding program used by the breeder in the first weeks of your Siberian's life. You and your veterinarian can include this input into decisions made about your pup's diet and vaccination regimen for the future. Your veterinarian will want to keep a copy of the documentation regarding clearances of the your puppy's parents from the presence of genetically based diseases. Also, bring a fresh sample of your pup's stool to this visit so that your veterinarian can make a microscopic check for the presence of internal parasites.

The Annual Wellness Checkup

An annual checkup is often the only time your primary care veterinarian will examine your healthy Siberian Husky. Therefore, plan to schedule an annual checkup with your veterinarian to discuss any health care issues and to develop a baseline medical history for your Siberian when he is free of serious diseases. For aging dogs, chronically ill dogs, and dogs who travel frequently, establishing a reliable medical history, supplemented with regular blood work, will help your Siberian to receive prompt and appropriate medical care at home or on the road.

As his owner, you know your dog better than anyone else. Be alert to signs that he is not in tip-top health, and discuss them with your veterinarian. Take advantage of the expertise resident in the high-quality health care team you have created for your Siberian Husky, and combine it with your own good instincts to determine the course of his health care.

Lumps and Bumps

Your veterinarian will palpate, or feel, your Siberian's entire body from nose to tail. He will check for lumps, bumps, areas of sensitivity or pain, and the presence of excess fat. He will evaluate the overall appearance of the dog, paying special attention to his weight and the condition of his coat and skin. Dog hair that has become dull, patchy, or changed in color signals physiological problems like glandular disorders. Dry, flaky skin, eruptions, or rashes may indicate allergies or dietary deficiencies.

Parasites

While evaluating your dog's outward appearance, the vet will check for the presence of external parasites, including fleas, ticks, and mites. These parasites carry serious diseases and cause unpleasant skin reactions, besides bothering your dog to distraction by triggering itchy skin. Prepare to discuss a variety of measures for flea and tick control with your veterinarian.

Bring a fresh stool sample from your Siberian to the annual checkup. A microscopic evaluation of your dog's fecal sample will reveal the presence of internal parasites, such as hookworms, roundworms, and whipworms. The eggs shed by these intestinal parasites are visible under the microscope and indicate the need for medication to rid the dog of them.

Defining the Veterinary Medicine Terms

Conventional, Orthodox, or Allopathic — The typical care provided by most American veterinarians, principally using pharmaceuticals, drugs, and surgery to treat illness. Goals of this approach include speed (fast healing), pain relief, and eliminating undesirable symptoms. Many conventional veterinary practices also address preventive care as it relates to things like intestinal parasite control, heartworm prevention, yearly health exams, nutrition counseling, prophylactic dental care, thyroid screens, wellness programs, and behavioral advice. This type of therapy performs well in emergency situations and when addressing serious, immediate threats to health, such as infection.

Holistic, Alternative, or Complementary — These terms include a wide variety of modalities whose treatments address the entire dog, including his physical body, environment, and temperament. Herbal medicine, chiropractic, homeopathy, acupuncture, massage, nutrition, aromatherapy, and other treatments make up this broad category. These therapies concentrate on helping the dog's body to heal itself, rather than on relieving symptoms of the disease. Used both as a complement and as an alternative to conventional care, these treatments work slowly but mostly without significant, unwanted side effects.

Traditional — Although commonly used to reference conventional or modern veterinary medicine, this term more properly defines the older, holistic therapies. Modern veterinary medical practices are quite new to the health care scene, so the term "traditional" is better reserved for the older, and sometimes ancient, veterinary therapies, like acupuncture.

Teeth and Gums

Your veterinarian will check the condition of your Siberian's teeth and gums for the presence of plaque, tartar, and periodontal disease, as well as for healthy pink gum color. (Redness indicates inflammation.) Gum disease threatens the health of many dogs by creating an environment in which harmful bacteria can multiply and launch into a dog's bloodstream to attack other areas of the body, especially the heart.

Just like people, dogs require professional teeth cleaning to prevent gum disease and tooth loss, even if you clean your dog's teeth regularly at home. However, if you do take the time to clean your Siberian's teeth at home, you will greatly reduce the number of times your dog must endure a professional dental cleaning under general anesthesia.

Ears

Your dog's ears will receive attention during this examination. The veterinarian will check your dog's ear "leather" for evidence of fly bites or scratches. She will examine the inside of the ear for the presence of ear mites or a yeast infection, especially if you live in a hot, humid area. Early detection of ear problems prevents any infections from becoming entrenched.

Toenails

A look at your Siberian's toenails will tell your veterinarian if they have grown too long and cause your dog's toes to turn sideways when he walks. The ability to use his feet correctly and without discomfort is crucial to his role as a sled-pulling dog. Also, toenails that impede the proper action of a dog's feet contribute to the appearance of significant structural problems later in life.

If your Siberian retains his dewclaws, the high first claw located on his leg, your veterinarian will make certain that the dewclaw nail has not become ingrown.

Heart and Lungs

Using a stethoscope, the vet will listen to your Siberian's heart and lungs. She will check for heart murmurs, a special concern for all working and sporting breeds like the Siberian Husky, and for

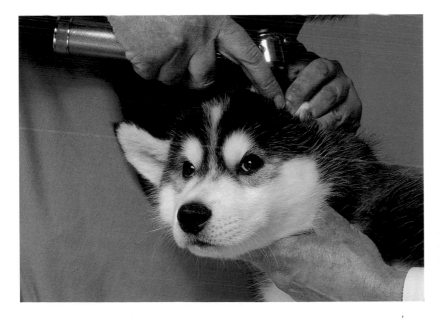

At his annual wellness checkup, the vet will examine your Siberian's ears.

the clarity of the dog's breathing.

Anal Glands

The canine anal glands are located on either side of the dog's anal opening and may become impacted or infected. Your veterinarian will check the health of these glands and "express," or remove, any fluid that appears to be backed up in them.

Structural Health

Watching your dog in motion will provide the vet with clues about his structural health. If your dog limps, moves in a sideways motion, has difficulty changing positions, or in any way seems to compensate for discomfort in his movements, your veterinarian may want to examine him further for skeletal or musculature problems.

ANNUAL CANINE VACCINATIONS

One of the most controversial topics in modern veterinary medicine is the advisability of administering annual vaccinations to our dogs. Veterinary medicine credits vaccinations with conquering some of the fiercest canine viral and infectious diseases. As a result, it established an annual vaccine protocol as a key element in a responsible owner's veterinary care regimen.

However, many health care professionals now suspect annual canine vaccines of creating long-term vulnerability to disease. Many veterinarians infer a link between annual vaccinations and chronic diseases like arthritis, seizures, allergies, skin conditions, gastrointestinal and thyroid disorders, immune system disorders, and cancer. Few veterinarians, no matter how holistic their leanings, advocate eliminating canine vaccinations altogether, though. Most recommend administering fewer vaccinations. In other words, veterinarians want to vaccinate dogs enough to prevent disease but not enough to cause disease.

Titer Tests

How can veterinarians and dog owners find the delicate balance between overvaccinating and undervaccinating a Siberian? A blood analysis called a "titer test" can help veterinarians and owners decide whether a dog requires a vaccination to boost immunity levels at any time in his life. The titer test can provide a basis for

Taking Your Dog's Temperature

Use a rectal thermometer lubricated with a water-based lubricating jelly, or an infrared ear thermometer, to take your Siberian's temperature. The normal canine temperature ranges between 100.5° and 103°F (38.1° and 39.4°C) but may vary with the temperature of the air. Become familiar with your dog's normal temperature in varying weather conditions, and record your findings. Changes in your Siberian's normal temperature based on the existing environment signal a cause for concern.

informed decisions about canine vaccinations, rather than relying on the old standard that if some vaccinating is good, more is better. Or even worse, relying on the manufacturer's recommended vaccination schedule rather than on the results of independent scientific research.

The term "titer" refers to the strength or concentration of a substance in solution. The canine titer test checks a sample of the dog's blood for the presence and strength of the dog's immunological response to a particular viral disease. If the dog's response proves satisfactory, the dog does not require further vaccination against that disease at that time.

By "titering" annually, an owner can assess whether her dog's immune response has fallen below an adequate level. In that event, a veterinarian should administer the appropriate vaccine booster.

Common Diseases to Protect Against

The following are some diseases against which many dogs are commonly vaccinated.

Bordetella (Kennel Cough)

A bacterial infection in the canine respiratory tract causes the chronic, dry cough commonly known as kennel cough. Some dogs also develop a nasal discharge. Transmission occurs easily among dogs living together in close quarters. A vaccination delivered intranasally or subcutaneously prevents the disease. Veterinarians will administer an antibiotic and recommend supportive care for dogs who have contracted kennel cough.

Coronavirus

A milder canine viral infection than parvovirus, coronavirus attacks the digestive tracts of younger dogs, causing mild diarrhea. A blood test is the only method of reliably distinguishing parvovirus from coronavirus. Care consists of administering fluids and supportive treatments.

Distemper

Distemper is the greatest single threat to the world's dog population. Younger dogs and puppies are most susceptible to this disease. Symptoms include discharge from the eyes, coughing, vomiting, listlessness, poor appetite, and diarrhea. In some cases,

the virus may infect the nervous system. Treatment includes antibiotics to prevent secondary infections, fluid therapy, and supportive care.

Leptospirosis

This bacterial disease impairs kidney function and is spread by contact with the urine of infected animals. Signs include poor appetite, lethargy, vomiting, depression, muscle pain, and sometimes seizures, diarrhea, or bloody urine. Your veterinarian will prescribe an antibiotic and supportive care.

Lyme Disease

Spread by the bite of a tick no larger than the head of a pin, Lyme disease is a bacterial infection that, if left untreated, can lead to joint, heart, and neurological damage. Symptoms are flu-like, including vomiting, lethargy, and weight loss. Your veterinarian may diagnose this condition through a blood test. In the early stages of the disease, antibiotics have proven effective. Chronic

Dogs are commonly vaccinated against a variety of diseases.

cases respond to treatment more slowly.

Parainfluenza

A virus causes this mild but contagious respiratory tract infection. Dogs with parainfluenza develop a cough, fever, and thick nasal discharge. Supportive care and treatment of any secondary bacterial infections are recommended.

Parvovirus

This viral infection attacks the canine intestinal tract, white blood cells, and even the heart. The first signs of parvovirus are depression, loss of appetite, vomiting, and extensive diarrhea, often containing blood. Early treatment with fluids and antibiotics to control secondary infections is critical to the dog's survival.

Rabies

Rabies is a contagious, fatal viral disease. Because most state laws require rabies vaccinations, owners may not be able to avoid administering regular rabies vaccinations to their dogs, even if a titer test indicates the presence of a satisfactory antibody level.

If your dog is currently in poor health, your local jurisdiction may accept a letter from your veterinarian stating that a rabies vaccination may cause your dog irreparable health problems. However, do not take this step lightly. If your Siberian does bite someone, the authorities may push to euthanize your dog and test him for rabies, even if you have a recent titer test that indicates your dog's satisfactory immunity level for this disease. Public health officials steer clear of exceptions and exemptions in matters of protecting the public from a serious viral disease.

Discuss the specific pros and cons of rabies vaccinations with your veterinarian, even if you are adamant about titer testing your Siberian Husky for immunity from other viral diseases.

EXTERNAL PARASITES

The fight against the invasion of external parasites continues to rage among dog owners. These small but extremely irritating pests cause skin problems ranging from minor itching to rashes, skin eruptions, open sores, skin infections, and other serious skin reactions. External parasites can also carry and spread diseases like Lyme disease, cause mange, and transmit other parasites, such as tapeworms.

In general, you can keep your Siberian Husky free of external parasites by taking these important steps:

1. Check for the presence of fleas, ticks, and coat and skin abnormalities each time you groom your Siberian.
2. With the guidance of your veterinary team, select the least toxic control program that does the job of eliminating the presence of parasites on your dog and in his environment.
3. Arrange for prompt veterinary treatment of your dog if he exhibits the signs of parasitic infection like excessive scratching, chewing on his skin and coat, licking, or shaking his head.
4. If you have more than one dog, check and treat all of them once one dog becomes infested.
5. Thoroughly steam clean your carpets, and vacuum and clean floors and furniture.

Safe Travel With Your Siberian Husky

A healthy, well-socialized, and well-trained Siberian Husky makes a wonderful travel companion. Your investment in your Siberian's early socialization and training will reap the rewards of a dog who functions well in unfamiliar surroundings and in the company of strangers.

Rely on the advice of your veterinary team about the fitness of your Siberian for travel, and don't travel with a physically ill or impaired dog. Prepare a travel kit for your pet, and take along supplies that will make your dog feel comfortable on the road. Include your canine first-aid kit or a modified version of it depending on the space available.

Before undertaking a trip, prepare to help your Siberian with the physical problems that beset many travelers, human and canine alike. Consult with your conventional and holistic veterinarian about remedies for carsickness, constipation, diarrhea, and anxiety. Many herbal and homeopathic remedies and flower essences offer gentle relief from these conditions without causing side effects. Also, perform a daily health check on your Siberian when you are away from home. Watch for unusual discharge from his nose or eyes, excessive scratching or biting at himself, abnormal elimination, and any lack of appetite or decreased energy level.

Try to stick to your normal feeding schedule, and take along a jug of water from home. If you do so, you will have water available for your dog at every stop, and water from home will cause your dog less digestive upset than water from other sources. Also, remember that a well-exercised dog is a good dog, at home or on the road. Although you will be busy with your travel activities, don't forget to provide daily exercise for your Siberian. You will both sleep more soundly!

6. Launder your Siberian's bedding material often, and dry the bedding in a hot dryer.

7. Use a flea comb to trap fleas on your dog and kill them immediately.

8. Mow your lawn, rake your leaves, and trim your shrubbery to allow sunlight to penetrate and warm the soil, which kills parasite larvae.

9. Do not use strong pesticides to kill all the insects in your yard. For example, ants eat flea eggs and larvae and help to maintain a balance in the environment.

Both conventional and holistic veterinary approaches offer a host of solutions for the treatment, control, and prevention of external parasites. When addressing pest control, find the path that leads to successfully curbing a parasite problem without jeopardizing your Siberian's overall good health.

Fleas

Fleas are black-brown in color and about the size of a sesame seed. They thrive in warm, humid weather and move rapidly over a dog's skin. Adult fleas live their entire lives on a dog, biting him to extract a "blood meal." Female fleas lay eggs that scatter around the dog's environment, including on his bedding, in carpets, on furniture, and in the grass and dirt where he spends time. The flea larvae emerge from their eggs and continue to infest him and the environment.

Some dogs develop an allergy to flea saliva, which compounds a dog's reactions to these parasites. Fleas can carry tapeworm larvae and pass them on to a dog who ingests a flea harboring these larvae. Heavily infested dogs can become anemic as a result of multiple flea bites.

Scratching at his itchy coat usually provides the first indication that fleas are pestering a dog. "Flea dirt," or the black droppings left by fleas on a dog's coat, signals the presence of fleas on a dog, sometimes before the owner discovers the fleas themselves.

Ticks

When dogs investigate shrubbery and bushes, piles of cut brush, and wild undergrowth, they may bring back unwanted hitchhikers: ticks. Ticks prefer to bite and attach to a dog on the neck, in the ears, in the folds of the skin, on the face, and between the toes.

Ticks spread a variety of infectious diseases that vary by region and by the tick species itself.

Check your Siberian often for the presence of these parasites, especially in tick-prone areas and during tick season, and after camping, hiking, or running your dog in sporting events in above-freezing climates.

Owners should remove ticks promptly to reduce the chance of disease transmission. Wear rubber gloves if possible. Use tweezers or a hemostat to firmly grasp the tick as close to the dog's skin as possible, and gently pull it free of his skin. After removing the tick, crush it, flush it down the toilet, and wash your hands thoroughly with soap and water. Treat the site of the bite with an antibiotic cream.

Mites

Ear mites are most common in young dogs. These microscopic pests infest the ear canal and cause itchy, infected ears. In advanced cases of mite infestation, the dog may scratch bleeding sores in his ears. Usually, a smelly, black ear discharge accompanies an ear mite infection. Cleaning and medicating infected ears eliminates the infestation.

Sarcoptic mange mites, which affect dogs during all seasons of the year, burrow through the outer layer of a dog's skin and cause intense itching. They are highly contagious and can pass from one dog to another through physical contact, bedding material, and grooming tools. Infected dogs lose hair and develop skin rashes and crusty patches on the skin. Veterinarians prescribe medications to kill the mites as well as to soothe the dog's skin and relieve any secondary skin infections.

Demodectic mange mites live in the follicles of most healthy dogs but may cause problems in certain individuals whose immune systems are ineffective in controlling normal populations of the mites in their skin. Adult-onset demodectic mange, while not contagious, is extremely serious and requires almost continual attention.

INTERNAL PARASITES

Parasites invade the digestive tract, blood vessels, and the heart. They live by taking vital nutrition from the dog. They may cause mild symptoms, or in advanced cases, they may cause death from blood loss or damage to internal organs.

Heartworms

Heartworms are long, spaghetti-like worms that inhabit and severely weaken a dog's heart and result in shortness of breath, coughing, lack of energy, and eventually, death. Because mosquitoes carry this disease, many owners discontinue preventive treatment for heartworm during the colder months of the year. However, the treatment for heartworm infestation is very hard on a dog, so maintain your Siberian on year-round preventive care unless you live in the very coldest winter climates. Also, heartworms can significantly damage a dog's heart before their presence is discovered, so allow your veterinarian to perform an annual blood test even if your Siberian receives preventive

treatment throughout the year.

Hookworms

Parasites of the small intestines, hookworms have large mouths with hook-like teeth that they use to attach themselves to the lining of a dog's small intestine, allowing them to suck blood for nutrition. Mild cases may not exhibit symptoms, but signs of advanced infestations include pale gums and tongue, dark stools, and a generally unhealthy appearance. Deworming medications dispensed by a veterinarian and supportive care will treat this condition.

Roundworms

Roundworms are relatively large intestinal parasites that can spread from dogs to humans. In advanced cases, they can cause distension of the abdomen because of their large size. Weakness and lack of appetite signal a roundworm infection, which can be treated with a prescription deworming medication.

Tapeworms

Tapeworm segments resemble flattened beads or grains of rice that are visible in a dog's stool. The dog must ingest a carrier, such as a rodent or a flea containing tapeworm larvae, to become infected. Sometimes, a dog will rub his bottom along the ground because of itching caused by tapeworm segments that have become stuck under his tail. The specific medication used to eliminate tapeworms depends on the type of tapeworm present in the dog.

Whipworms

Whipworms invade a dog's large intestines and cause bloody diarrhea and general debilitation. Deworming medication eliminates the condition, but careful cleaning of the dog's environment to prevent reinfestation is necessary.

COMMON HEALTH CONCERNS

No breed remains entirely free from inherited defects, but few breeds have the good fortune of the Siberian Husky. The majority of individuals enjoy good health, freedom from inherited defects, and lovely temperaments, even after years of explosive growth in the breed. Nevertheless, Siberians do suffer from a higher than

Identifying Genetically Based Health Problems

Since 1965, the SHCA has maintained a committee dedicated to the task of identifying the first indications of the presence of genetically based problems in the breed. The committee alerts breeders to the potential dangers of any defect before it spreads throughout the general Siberian breeding population.

average incidence of epilepsy, certain eye diseases, hip dysplasia, hypothyroidism, osteochondrosis, and von Willebrand's disease. Other general diseases that may affect your Siberian (but to which they are not genetically predisposed) include allergies, bloat, and cancer.

Allergies

Allergies are severe reactions of the dog's immune system to various external conditions that include food substances, insect bites, and environmental factors like lawn chemicals, pollen, and smog.

Symptoms

Red, irritated, and blotchy skin that seems itchy to the dog signals the presence of an allergic condition. Also, the dog may experience patchy hair loss, sneezing, and may bite at his own skin.

Treatment

Work with your veterinarian to provide relief of symptoms while determining the cause of the allergic reaction. Consider nutritional supplements like fatty acids to improve skin condition and vitamin C to improve immunological response. Also, keep your dog's environment as clean as possible.

Bloat

Bloat is a veterinary emergency of the highest order and a condition for which there are no home remedies. It affects as many as 60,000 dogs per year and has a fatality rate of up to 33 percent. Sadly, bloat continues its reign as a top killer of companion dogs, especially the larger deep-chested breeds. However, even small dogs fall victim to this condition.

When bloat occurs, gas and occasionally fluids accumulate in the dog's stomach, causing it to dilate. Dilation alone can occur, or it can be the first step leading to torsion, the rotation and twisting of the stomach. The expanded stomach puts pressure on several large arteries and veins, constricting the vital flow of blood to the stomach and other areas of the dog's body. A lack of blood supply can lead to tissue damage and the buildup of toxic materials in the stomach and body. Bloat is a life-threatening emergency that requires rapid intervention from a veterinary surgeon.

What Causes Bloat?

Some factors appear to increase the risk of bloat, but a definitive answer to the question of what causes this condition still eludes veterinary science. The most widely accepted risk factor is the anatomy of the dog. Large, deep-chested breeds tend to bloat more often than other breeds. The risk of bloat seems to increase with age, perhaps due to the weakening of the ligaments that hold the stomach in place over time. Having a close relative who has experienced bloat contributes to the risk, so always consult your Siberian Husky breeder about the incidence of bloat, if any, in the breeding line. Stressed dogs and dogs with fearful personalities also may bloat more frequently than confident, well-adjusted dogs. Dogs who eat only one large meal a day and who tend to rapidly gulp their food are more at risk for bloat. Some veterinarians also believe that dogs who eat dry food are more prone to bloat. A recent study suggests that feeding a dog from a bowl elevated on a stand or rack seemed to increase the risk of bloat. Contrary to commonly held beliefs, no definitive connection has been made between eating and drinking before or after exercise as a risk factor. However, as a safety precaution, allow your dog to warm up before exercising and cool down afterward, and don't feed him a large meal directly before or after an exercise session.

Symptoms

Learn to recognize the symptoms of bloat, some of which may be subtle, and seek emergency veterinary care immediately:

- continual pacing, restlessness
- salivating, panting, whining, excessive drooling
- unproductive or frothy vomiting
- acting agitated, distressed, can't get comfortable
- swollen or distended abdomen, stomach taut to the touch
- repeatedly turning to look at flank or abdomen

Treatment

At first, your veterinarian may pass a tube into your Siberian's stomach to relieve the pressure. In almost all cases, a veterinary surgeon will perform a gastropexy, or the surgical repositioning of the stomach and the immobilization, or "tacking," of the stomach to the abdominal wall. Dogs who have undergone gastropexy may experience gastric dilation in the future, but their stomach will no longer be able to rotate.

Dogs who have been properly treated for bloat have a greater than 80 percent chance of surviving and leading a normal life. However, a successful outcome hinges on swift treatment.

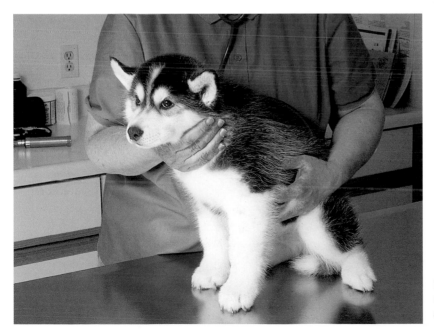

Take your Siberian to the vet if you feel any suspicious lumps or bumps.

Cancer

Cancer occurs in dogs when the normal genes within each cell that control growth fail, and the cell divides rapidly and relentlessly—literally "out of control." Normally, a dog's healing system eliminates cells that contain damaged or altered genes. Therefore, cancer represents a failure of a dog's immune system, at least with respect to the cancerous cells.

Treating Cancer

Make any treatment decisions based primarily on the quality of life that they offer your Siberian in the short and long term.

What Causes Cancer?

Many factors can contribute to this healing system crisis in a dog. They include external factors such as pollution, poor nutrition, poor emotional health, stress and anxiety, exposure to toxic chemicals, overvaccination, and others. Veterinarians refer to cancers initiated by these external factors as "acquired cancers." When a dog inherits a predisposition to cancer due to the gene profile that he inherited from his sire and dam, veterinarians term the resulting disease "inherited cancer."

Symptoms

The following are the American Veterinary Medical Association's (AVMA) ten common signs of cancer:

- abnormal swellings that persist or continue to grow
- bleeding or discharge from any body opening
- difficulty breathing, urinating, or defecating
- difficulty eating or swallowing
- hesitation to exercise or loss of stamina
- loss of appetite
- offensive body odor
- persistent lameness or stiffness
- sores that do not heal
- weight loss

Treatment

Conventional and traditional veterinary protocols offer many treatment options for canine cancer. Siberian Husky owners who must develop a cancer treatment program for their dog should immediately enlist the aid of their entire veterinary team to create a plan of attack designed specifically for the needs of their dog.

Surgery, chemotherapy, and radiation therapy compose the most common conventional approaches to cancer treatment. Surgery, especially for localized tumors situated in an area appropriate for surgical intervention, remains the first choice for treatment. Cancer found in the heart wall, for instance, or scattered in several different areas of the body may respond better to chemotherapy or toxic agents used to kill cancer cells. When the cancer exists as a solitary nodule in the body, a veterinarian may use a focused beam of radiation to target and kill the cancer cells at the site.

Most cases of spontaneous remission have occurred when the dog's immune system becomes activated to clear out the cancer. Holistic veterinary methods support this process of boosting the dog's own immune system to do its work. Feeding a highly nutritious, low-carbohydrate diet is a great place to begin holistic therapy. Cancer cells feed on carbohydrates. Many holistic veterinarians recommend dietary supplements like shark cartilage, vitamin C, and other immunostimulants. Western and Chinese herbal remedies, acupuncture, and enzyme therapy also help to bolster a dog's immune system.

As always, reducing the risk factors for this deadly disease deserves serious consideration. Incorporate these cancer prevention practices into your Siberian Husky's daily care regimen:

- Feed a properly balanced and nutritious diet free of pesticides and preservatives.
- Provide pure drinking water.
- Supplement his diet with antioxidants, enzymes, vitamins, and minerals as needed.
- Provide regular training and exercise.
- Be mindful of your Siberian's emotional well-being; eliminate stress and anxiety.
- Titer test for the presence of proper immunologic response to canine viral diseases; vaccinate only when necessary.
- Neuter nonbreeding stock.
- Eliminate the use of toxic chemicals, like lawn pesticides, in your Siberian's environment.

A world of information exists about the wide variety of treatments available for canine cancer. Inform yourself about the options, and enlist the expertise of your veterinary team to mount your battle against this dreaded disease.

Epilepsy

Epilepsy is caused by abnormal brain activity and results in

Siberian Huskies are prone to bilateral cataracts, crystalline corneal opacities, and progressive retinal atrophy.

seizures. Some forms of epilepsy have a genetic foundation, while others may be triggered by environmental factors, like toxins.

Symptoms

Seizures usually occur when the dog is quiet. He may stiffen, urinate, defecate, drool, work his jaws, or thrash his limbs uncontrollably. Dogs usually appear disoriented after the seizure has passed.

Treatment

Keep a record of any seizure activity in your dog. Your veterinarian will consider the frequency and severity of the seizures when prescribing treatment, including antiseizure medication.

Eye Diseases

Three genetically based diseases of the eye afflict the Siberian Husky: bilateral cataracts, crystalline corneal opacities, and progressive retinal atrophy (PRA). Each disease attacks a different portion of the eye. These conditions occur in both male and female Siberians, regardless of eye color. The eye diseases discussed in this section result in conditions that range from a loss of visual acuity to blindness.

Bilateral Cataracts

Bilateral cataracts manifest as a cloudiness of the lens of the eye in a relatively young dog. Sometimes they are called "juvenile cataracts" to distinguish them from cataracts that occur in senior dogs as a normal result of aging, or cataracts that result from an injury to a dog's eye. Occasionally, bilateral cataracts become apparent in one eye several months before the other eye shows any symptoms. The clouding of the lens of the dog's eye may become so severe as to result in blindness. Surgical removal of juvenile cataracts and other genetically based cataracts usually produces good results.

Crystalline Corneal Opacities

Crystalline corneal opacities produce a gray haze or needle-like crystals within the cornea that spread across the surface of the cornea and obscure vision. Usually, both eyes are affected, but not necessarily at the same time or to the same degree. The onset of the disease can occur when a pup is only several months old or when a dog reaches several years of age. There is no definitive cure for this condition.

Progressive Retinal Atrophy (PRA)

PRA affects the light-sensitive rods and cones in the retina of a dog's eye. Some types of this disease cause the dog to lose night vision, which then degenerates into a loss of day vision as well. Other types cause the dog to see better in dim light than in bright light. He can develop a blind spot in his central field of vision and may bump into stationary objects while distinguishing moving objects quite clearly. Age of onset of PRA varies from a few weeks to several years and may result in a severely handicapped dog due to his diminished or complete loss of vision. The incidence of PRA in the Siberian Husky is very low. There is no definitive cure for this disease.

How Are Eye Defects Diagnosed?

Accurate diagnosis of inherited eye defects requires the expertise of a veterinary ophthalmologist. Many local Siberian Husky clubs sponsor such eye exams annually, making them readily available to breeders throughout the country. The examination is simple and painless. The precise mode of transmission of inherited canine eye diseases from one generation to the next is unknown, so careful examination of the eyes of dogs in a breeding kennel has become an annual event for conscientious breeders.

Hip Dysplasia

Hip dysplasia is an abnormality of the hip joint in which the head of the dog's thighbone does not fit properly into his pelvic joint socket. This defect is rarely present at birth, and it develops during the first two years of life.

Siberian Husky breeders estimate that about 5 to 10 percent of the breed is afflicted with hip dysplasia, ranging from a slight to a severe degree of involvement. Compared to the 40 to 50 percent rates of affliction in some dog breeds, Siberian Husky breeders consider hip dysplasia to be a source of great concern but not a health care emergency for the breed.

What Causes Hip Dysplasia?

Although nothing can change the underlying genetic component of hip dysplasia, environmental elements play a significant role in the severity of the disease. Factors such as insufficient exercise, prolonged and extremely vigorous exercise, inadequate nutrition, and rapid weight gain increase the degree to which the disease affects an individual dog.

Removing dogs who carry any of the genes attributed to canine hip dysplasia from a breeding program is the only method of preventing the appearance of the disease in future generations. The SHCA's breeding guidelines suggest that breeders clear the parents, grandparents, and close relatives of a stud dog or brood bitch from the presence of hip dysplasia before entering him or her in a breeding program.

A radiographic examination of an individual dog's hips when he is at least two years old is the only reliable method of acquiring an accurate diagnosis of hip dysplasia. Breeders and owners may not be able to identify young, slightly dysplastic dogs any other way. A veterinarian sedates the dog, which allows his rear limbs to relax, extend, and be placed and held in a very specific position. The vet then takes an X-ray of the dog's hips and submits it to a veterinary radiologist for diagnosis.

Symptoms

A progressive disease, hip dysplasia causes inflammation, pain, and early-onset arthritis in the dog's hip. In slight to moderate cases affecting younger dogs, strenuous exercise temporarily aggravates the condition. In moderate to severe cases, and in older dogs, the dog cannot negotiate stairs and has difficulty rising from a sitting or a prone position.

Hip dysplasia affects male and female dogs alike and more commonly impacts larger breeds of dog. Because owners of the Siberian Husky prize their dogs' fluid, effortless movement when running freely or when pulling a sled, this structural disease represents a major concern for all Siberian breeders.

Treatment

Treatments vary from conditioning to improve the ability of the surrounding muscle to support a dysplastic hip joint, to the surgical correction or replacement of the joint.

Hypothyroidism

Hypothyroidism is the undersecretion of the thyroid hormone by a dog's thyroid gland.

Promote good health in your Siberian by ensuring that he receives the proper amount of exercise.

Symptoms

Lethargy, weight gain, skin problems, and a dull coat are signals that your dog may be suffering from this condition.

Treatment

With the administration of proper medication to return the dog's thyroid level to normal, as well as the use of holistic therapies like acupuncture, the symptoms may quickly disappear.

FIRST AID FOR YOUR SIBERIAN HUSKY

Be prepared to administer a minimal amount of first aid to your dog in the first few minutes of a medical emergency. Then, prepare your dog for transport, and bring him to a veterinary facility immediately. First-aid procedures are temporary measures to use while contacting a veterinarian and readying transportation for your dog. Use them to stabilize and to protect him from further injury. Do not rely on first aid to delay or replace emergency veterinary care or as a prolonged treatment regimen for any medical condition.

Plan ahead and assemble a canine first-aid kit. Keep the telephone numbers and directions of your veterinarians, emergency veterinary clinics, and poison control centers at hand.

The Canine First-Aid Kit

Include the following items in your canine first-aid kit:

- antibiotic ointment
- antidiarrhea medicine
- bandage scissors
- Benadryl capsules
- booties
- bottled water
- buffered aspirin
- documentation: dog's medication records, poison control telephone numbers, regular and emergency veterinary clinic telephone numbers and hours of operation
- eye wash (saline solution in a squirt bottle)
- gauze sponges
- hemostat
- holistic remedies (Rescue Remedy, herbal remedies)
- hydrocortisone cream
- hydrogen peroxide
- liquid medicinal soap
- material to use as splints
- rubbing alcohol
- small plastic bags
- soft muzzle
- sterile stretch gauze pads
- sterile, nonadherent pads
- thermometer
- towels
- tweezers
- vet wrap self-adhesive bandage roll

If your injured dog appears so upset as to be likely to bite due to overexcitement or pain, cover his head with a blanket or towel, or place a soft muzzle on him before handling him. If your dog has difficulty breathing, appears to be about to vomit, or does vomit, do not use a muzzle, or immediately remove one already in place. Never leave an unattended dog muzzled.

Evaluate your dog's level of consciousness and breathing, and listen for a heartbeat, if possible. Check his eyes, ears, nose, chest, abdomen, back, and limbs, and take his temperature. Telephone the veterinary clinic where you will bring your dog, and report your findings about his condition right away. Any information that you can provide in advance of your arrival at the veterinary clinic will aid the staff with its preparations for treating your dog.

Head, Neck, and Back Injuries

If you find evidence of a head, neck, or back injury, or your dog seems unable to move his rear legs, do not pick him up or carry him. Slide him onto a flat surface for transportation to a veterinary facility.

Prolonged exposure to the cold can result in frostbite.

Wounds

Wash your hands and any instruments you use before handling a dog with a wound or cut. First, stop any bleeding, and then work to prevent infection. Irrigate a wound with clean drinking water, or wash it carefully with a medicinal soap. Carefully clip the dog's hair away from the edge of the wound. Apply an antibiotic ointment. Administer any holistic remedies as recommended by your holistic veterinarian. Bandage the wound if necessary. Don't wipe a wound that has stopped bleeding, or you may dislodge a blood clot.

Heatstroke

Dogs cool themselves by panting, which is a relatively inefficient method of temperature control. In fact, they do not tolerate high temperatures as well as humans and suffer from heatstroke much more easily than their owners. In the case of heatstroke, immediately reduce your dog's temperature by immersing him in a cool bath or using a garden hose to wet him down. Make sure that the water reaches the dog's skin and stays cool. Consult with your veterinarian immediately.

Frostbite

Prolonged exposure to the cold results in a dangerous drop in body temperature. Fortunately, the highly effective Siberian Husky coat protects him from extremely cold temperatures. However, frostbite can affect a dog's toes, ears, and scrotum. At first, the skin appears pale and white; then it swells and changes to bright red when circulation returns. Apply warm water soaks to any affected areas, and seek veterinary care.

To help to prevent frostbite, use canine booties when participating in cold-temperature sports.

THE INTEGRATIVE APPROACH TO CANINE HEALTH CARE

Illness is rarely caused by just one factor, and illness rarely impacts only one portion of a living being. Holistic practitioners treat a health problem in its entirety and treat the animal patient as a whole. Holistic methods attempt to produce deep, inner healing rather than merely providing symptom repression.

As in human medicine, holistic health care "modalities" or practices have attracted much attention in recent years. Modern veterinary medicine, with its powerful pharmaceuticals and advanced surgical techniques, swept venerable holistic treatments such as herbal remedies and homeopathy into a dark and quiet corner of the medicine cabinet. However, these traditional treatments, accompanied by newer holistic modalities, have emerged again as a distinctly beneficial complement to today's mainstream medical practices, offering additional, valuable resources for achieving genuine healing and improving the overall health of your dog.

Why Use Holistic Modalities?

Most holistic modalities address the mental well-being of the

When It's an Emergency

Don't hesitate! Some crisis conditions require immediate emergency veterinary care:

- bloat
- bruising blows or trauma to the torso that may have initiated internal bleeding
- burns
- continual coughing, sneezing, snorting, or difficulty breathing
- convulsions or unexpected seizures
- elevated body temperature
- fractured or broken bones
- heatstroke and heat exhaustion
- poisoning
- severe wounds, deep cuts, or profuse bleeding
- shock
- snake bite or poisonous spider bite
- swelling, discharge from, or injury to the eye

dog in their evaluation and treatment programs. Dogs exhibit a wide range of emotions, or responses, to their environment based on their feelings. Stress, emotional upset, turmoil, or the serious illness of a human family member can produce negative health consequences in dogs that include diarrhea, skin eruptions, and other conditions that defy identification and successful treatment through conventional medical examination. However, the holistic veterinary model contains homeopathic and herbal remedies and even nutritional programs that help a dog to deal with these environmental stress factors and gradually achieve healing.

Think about the following aspects of your choice of canine health care therapies, and keep your options open by integrating conventional veterinary care with holistic treatments:

- **Safety:** Get and keep your dog well using the safest possible treatment, with the fewest side effects and the least invasive procedures. Know exactly what you are treating whenever possible.
- **Effectiveness:** Select and combine therapies that heal disease rather than mask symptoms. Use the best of both holistic

and conventional veterinary medicine to attack disease while supporting your dog's overall health and ability to mount his own response to illness.

- **Speed:** Turn to conventional veterinary care for a quick response to emergency and life-threatening situations like infections or broken bones. Consider holistic veterinary care for the long-term healing of chronic diseases like allergies or digestive problems.

Identifying the Members of Your Integrated Health Care Team

Nutritional specialties involve building health through food choices and dietary supplementation.

Some veterinary clinics offer the services of both conventional and holistic veterinarians in one practice. Other conventional clinics provide a curt nod to holistic modalities to attract clients who have heard about the healing capabilities of holistic medicine. Such a practice may include many conventional veterinarians and one veterinarian who has taken courses in canine chiropractic, for instance. Single clinics that offer a wide range of conventional and holistic treatments tend to be a rare exception to the rule. In most cases, you will have to create your own team of veterinary

medicine practitioners willing to participate in an open dialogue and work together with you and their colleagues to support the health of your Siberian.

Choose each caregiver for her ability to communicate clearly and openly with you and other medical professionals. Select a conventional vet with whom you can be frank about any of your plans for holistic care. Find a holistic veterinarian who recognizes the value in the information provided by conventional diagnostic procedures, like blood tests, and who will use holistic therapies to support conventional procedures like setting broken bones or surgical interventions. Identify both the strengths and limitations in each veterinary practice that you select.

Remain informed and open minded, and put together a high-quality health care team for your Siberian Husky well before your dog faces serious health care concerns.

The Foundational Holistic Modalities

The foundation of holistic canine health care and medicine includes the specific specialties of acupuncture, chiropractic, herbal therapy, homeopathy, and nutrition. Cover these bases when you add a holistic practitioner to your Siberian's health care team. (Other modalities like massage, flower essences, TTouch, and aromatherapy represent simpler health care treatments that owners can often learn and practice themselves.)

Acupuncture

With acupuncture therapy, skilled therapists insert extremely fine needles at the site of critical points that control the flow of energy in a dog's body. The stimulation provided by the needles corrects any excesses or deficiencies in the energy flow, which supports health and healing. In fact, acupuncture fine-tunes the energy flow within your Siberian's body, correcting any energy blockages and allowing healing energy to efficiently travel to the sites of compromised health. Many acupuncturists require a dog to undergo a chiropractic adjustment before receiving an acupuncture treatment.

Chiropractic Treatment

Also referred to as biomechanical therapy, chiropractic therapy involves manually checking a dog's skeletal structure for

Helping the Flow of *Qi*

Some holistic veterinary therapies, like acupuncture and chiropractic, are sometimes referred to as "energy therapies" because they assist with the flow of the dog's natural energy throughout the body, called "qi" (pronounced "chee"). This energy runs along channels, called meridians, that occur in patterns along a dog's body, just like water flows in a system of streambeds to larger rivers. The energy therapies remove obstructions and balance disturbances in the flow of "qi", thereby encouraging the dog's body to send its healing powers effectively to the site of disease. As a group of therapies that enhance normal body functions like digestion and energy production, they also act as powerful disease preventives.

A good preventive care plan will help to keep your Siberian healthy for years to come.

misalignments of the bones and joints (called "subluxations"), places where the joints are stuck or loose, and the range of motion of each of the joints. Canine chiropractors manually adjust the dog's skeletal structure to eliminate dysfunctions and return the dog's structure to normal. A properly aligned physical structure allows for the uninterrupted flow of healing energy throughout your Siberian's body.

Herbs

Herbal medicines use the complex properties of specific plants to assist with healing and strengthening the dog's own immune system.

Homeopathy

Using extremely dilute solutions of natural substances, like plant derivatives or minerals, homeopathy stimulates the body's natural healing energy. A properly chosen homeopathic remedy relies on the free-flowing energy of a dog's body to carry it to the site of disease and initiate the dog's own healing response.

Nutrition

Nutritional specialties involve building health and supporting healing through food choices and dietary supplementation. In fact, proper nutrition underlies the overall health of your Siberian, both in a preventive role and in a healing role. Start with a high-quality diet and supplementation to help your dog develop optimum health or recover from disease.

With his confident carriage, his coat like a shining cloud, and all parts of his structure contributing to a picture of grace and fluidity, the Siberian Husky continues to inspire his many enthusiasts. Your attention to your Siberian Husky's good health throughout his lifetime will reward you with an opportunity to enjoy this fine breed as a physically sound and fit member of your family for many years.

ASSOCIATIONS AND ORGANIZATIONS

BREED CLUBS

American Kennel Club (AKC)
5580 Centerview Drive
Raleigh, NC 27606
Telephone: (919) 233-9767
Fax: (919) 233-3627
E-mail: info@akc.org
www.akc.org

Canadian Kennel Club (CKC)
89 Skyway Avenue, Suite 100
Etobicoke, Ontario M9W 6R4
Telephone: (416) 675-5511
Fax: (416) 675-6506
E-mail: information@ckc.ca
www.ckc.ca

Siberian Husky Club of America, Inc. (SHCA)
Corresponding Secretary: Julia Rylander
E-mail: SHCAinfo@msn.com
www.shca.org

The Kennel Club
1 Clarges Street
London
W1J 8AB
Telephone: 0870 606 6750
Fax: 0207 518 1058
www.the-kennel-club.org.uk

The Siberian Husky Club of Great Britain
E-mail: secretary@siberianhuskyclub.com
www.siberianhuskyclub.com

United Kennel Club (UKC)
100 E. Kilgore Road
Kalamazoo, MI 49002-5584
Telephone: (269) 343-9020
Fax: (269) 343-7037
E-mail: pbickell@ukcdogs.com
www.ukcdogs.com

RESCUE ORGANIZATIONS AND ANIMAL WELFARE GROUPS

American Humane Association (AHA)

63 Inverness Drive East

Englewood, CO 80112

Telephone: (303) 792-9900

Fax: 792-5333

www.americanhumane.org

American Society for the Prevention of Cruelty to Animals (ASPCA)

424 E. 92nd Street

New York, NY 10128-6804

Telephone: (212) 876-7700

www.aspca.org

Royal Society for the Prevention of Cruelty to Animals (RSPCA)

Telephone: 0870 3335 999

Fax: 0870 7530 284

www.rspca.org.uk

The Humane Society of the United States (HSUS)

2100 L Street, NW

Washington DC 20037

Telephone: (202) 452-1100

www.hsus.org

SPORTS

Canine Freestyle Federation, Inc.

Membership Secretary: Brandy Clymire

E-mail: CFFmemberinfo@aol.com

www.canine-freestyle.org

International Agility Link (IAL)

Global Administrator: Steve Drinkwater

E-mail: yunde@powerup.au

www.agilityclick.com/~ial

Sled Dog Central

www.sleddogcentral.com

VETERINARY RESOURCES

Academy of Veterinary Homeopathy (AVH)

P.O. Box 9280
Wilmington, DE 19809
Telephone: (866) 652-1590
Fax: (866) 652-1590
E-mail: office@TheAVH.org
www.theavh.org

American Academy of Veterinary Acupuncture (AAVA)

100 Roscommon Drive, Suite 320
Middletown, CT 06457
Telephone: (860) 635-6300
Fax: (860) 635-6400
E-mail: office@aava.org
www.aava.org

American Animal Hospital Association (AAHA)

P.O. Box 150899
Denver, CO 80215-0899
Telephone: (303) 986-2800
Fax: (303) 986-1700
E-mail: info@aahanet.org
www.aahanet.org/index.cfm

American Holistic Veterinary Medical Association (AHVMA)

2218 Old Emmorton Road
Bel Air, MD 21015
Telephone: (410) 569-0795
Fax: (410) 569-2346
E-mail: office@ahvma.org
www.ahvma.org

American Veterinary Medical Association (AVMA)

1931 North Meacham Road – Suite 100
Schaumburg, IL 60173
Telephone: (847) 925-8070
Fax: (847) 925-1329
E-mail: avmainfo@avma.org
www.avma.org

British Veterinary Association (BVA)

7 Mansfield Street
London
W1G 9NQ
Telephone: 020 7636 6541
Fax: 020 7436 2970
E-mail: bvahq@bva.co.uk
www.bva.co.uk

MISCELLANEOUS

Association of Pet Dog Trainers (APDT)

150 Executive Center Drive Box 35

Greenville, SC 29615

Telephone: (800) PET-DOGS

Fax: (864) 331-0767

E-mail: information@apdt.com

www.apdt.com

Delta Society

875 124th Ave NE, Suite 101

Bellevue, WA 98005

Telephone: (425) 226-7357

Fax: (425) 235-1076

E-mail: info@deltasociety.org

www.deltasociety.org

Therapy Dogs International (TDI)

88 Bartley Road
Flanders, NJ 07836

Telephone: (973) 252-9800

Fax: (973) 252-7171

E-mail: tdi@gti.net

www.tdi-dog.org

PUBLICATIONS

BOOKS

Lane, Dick, and Neil Ewart. *A-Z of Dog Diseases & Health Problems.* New York: Howell Books, 1997.

Rubenstein, Eliza, and Shari Kalina. *The Adoption Option: Choosing and Raising the Shelter Dog for You.* New York: Howell Books, 1996.

Serpell, James. *The Domestic Dog: Its Evolution, Behaviour and Interactions with People.* Cambridge: Cambridge University Press, 1995.

MAGAZINES

AKC Family Dog
American Kennel Club
260 Madison Avenue
New York, NY 10016
Telephone: (800) 490-5675
E-mail: familydog@akc.org
www.akc.org/pubs/familydog

AKC Gazette
American Kennel Club
260 Madison Avenue
New York, NY 10016
Telephone: (800) 533-7323
E-mail: gazette@akc.org
www.akc.org/pubs/gazette

Dog & Kennel
Pet Publishing, Inc.
7-L Dundas Circle
Greensboro, NC 27407
Telephone: (336) 292-4272
Fax: (336) 292-4272
E-mail: info@petpublishing.com
www.dogandkennel.com

Dog Fancy
Subscription Department
P.O. Box 53264
Boulder, CO 80322-3264
Telephone: (800) 365-4421
E-mail: barkback@dogfancy.com
www.dogfancy.com

Dogs Monthly
Ascot House
High Street, Ascot,
Berkshire SL5 7JG
United Kingdom
Telephone: 0870 730 8433
Fax: 0870 730 8431
E-mail: admin@rtc-associates.freeserve.co.uk
www.corsini.co.uk/dogsmonthly

WEBSITES

Dog-Play

www.dog-play.com/ethics.html

A cornucopia of information and pertinent links on responsible dog breeding.

The Dog Speaks

www.thedogspeaks.com

Canine behaviorist Deb Duncan's site, filled with useful advice on canine etiquette, behavior problems, communication, and relevant links.

Petfinder

www.petfinder.org

Search shelters and rescue groups for adoptable pets.

INDEX

PHOTO CREDITS

Photo on page 90 courtesy of Paulette Braun.
Photo on page 6 courtesy of pixshots (Shutterstock).
Photo on page 140 courtesy of Lara Stern.
All other photos courtesy of Isabelle Francais and T.F.H. archives.

Nylabone® Cares.

Millions of dogs of all ages, breeds, and sizes have enjoyed our world-famous chew bones—but we're not just bones! Nylabone®, the leader in responsible animal care for over 50 years, devotes the same care and attention to our many other award-winning, high-quality, innovative products. Your dog will love them — and so will you!

Toys   Treats   Chews   Crates   Grooming

Available at retailers everywhere. Visit us online at www.nylabone.com

DEDICATION

To my husband, Ralph, who has supported my life with dogs from day one.

ACKNOWLEDGMENTS

Many thanks to the members of the Siberian Husky Club of America (SHCA), the guardians of this magnificent dog breed, who generously shared their expertise, enthusiasm, and concerns about the breed.

ABOUT THE AUTHOR

Lorie Long has been raising and training purebred dogs for more than 25 years. She is a member and instructor at the Star City Canine Training Club in Roanoke, Virginia. She and her two Border Terriers regularly compete in the sport of dog agility. Lorie is a member of the Border Terrier Club of America. A member of the Dog Writers Association of America, she has written extensively for *The Whole Dog Journal*. She has been published in *Dog World* magazine and has written about safe boating with dogs for *Chesapeake Bay* magazine. While living in northern Virginia, Lorie served in several Board of Director positions, including club president for the Dulles Gateway Obedience Training Club. Lorie is also an award-winning freelance business writer.